Supported Living

-

Jodi's Journey Moves On

(A Disability Awareness and Inclusion Book)

Jean Shaw

Copyright

Supported Living - Jodi's Journey Moves On (A Disability Awareness Book)

Disclaimer

The information in this book is for educational purposes only.

The Author and Publisher has strived to be as accurate and complete as possible in the creation of this book. While all attempts have been made to verify information provided in this publication, the Author and Publisher assumes no responsibility for errors, omissions, or contrary interpretation of the subject matter herein.

Any perceived slights of specific persons, peoples, or organizations are unintentional.

Table Of Contents

Dedication

This book is dedicated to Cambs County Council and all the wonderful support staff who have made living independently possible for Jodi, Ben and Alex who all have learning difficulties and special needs.

Thanks also to Amy and Lucie.

Endorsement

Supported Living - Jodi's Journey Moves On is a look at autism from a unique perspective--that of a fly on the wall.

We walk through life with Jodi and his friends as they show that just because they are differently abled, that doesn't mean they can't experience life to the fullest.

Through the eyes of Flippin' the Fly, we tag along as Jodi attends woodworking class, learns to cook, and takes care of the garden. Though Flippin' brings an unusual perspective to the story, Jodi and his friends are clearly the stars of the show!

This book was written in such a way that older children can gain an understanding of what it might be like to live with a disability. However, it is a great read for adults as well.

As the parent of a child with autism, I related to Jodi's story on a personal level. Anyone who knows a person with a disability should read this book. It sheds new light on the idea that different is "extra-"ordinary.

--ID Johnson author of The Journey to Normal: Our Family's Life with Autism

Foreword

I don't know whether you've been following my son Jodi's journey or not, but this is the fourth book I've written about his life with autism. However, this is totally different from all the others, and truthfully has been the hardest for me to write.

The first book, **I'm Not Naughty, I'm Autistic - Jodi's Journey**, is about the first 11 years of his life, and was written as though Jodi was the narrator, which of course is ridiculous as he doesn't really speak. He says the occasional word, but never uses full sentences.

The second book, **Autism, Amalgam and Me - Jodi's Journey Continues**, covers why I think he has autism and what led me to that opinion. It tells my story and continues with his, so that book is written in two different voices; Jodi's and my own.

The third book, **Mercury Poisoning It's Not In Our Heads Anymore - Jodi's Journey Goes On**, has a clue in the title as to what it's about, but that one was written solely in my voice. It continues Jodi's journey but has the personal stories of many other individuals in it as well.

Now, as the years have passed, people are curious and have started asking,

"What happened to Jodi?"

That's because I tried to make my first book as humorous as possible, but ended it with these words:

"When autism struck my beautiful little boy it ruined his life and the ripple effects spread throughout our family. Fortunately, we are strong, but many families break under the strain.

It is hard to fight something you cannot see, but you must never give up hope.

Jodi is a fine looking youth, and I'm sure he will make a handsome man. We accept him as he is, but society is less tolerant of adults with strange behaviours than they are of cute little children.

We worry for his future and what will become of him.

As I said there's nothing funny about autism."

Hence this book!

Jodi is now grown up, and the problem I've had is determining whose "voice" to write this story in.

Who would be telling the tale?

You see, Jodi no longer lives at our family home. I don't see as much of him as I used to, and whilst we're in regular contact and I know what he's up to, most of the detail in this book comes from third party feedback.

It would be impossible to write in either Jodi's or my voice without doing a lot of guesswork, so as an experiment I'm using a totally different voice.

This time the voice is that of a ...

... fly!

Yes, I'm going to be a fly on the wall, and hopefully you'll appreciate the content Flippin the Fly is about to impart in this book, -

Supported Living - Jodi's Journey Moves On.

Of course, it's part truth and part fiction, which is totally different from the previous three books, but it's educational and does let the reader know Jodi is doing really well, much better than I ever dared hope!

Oh, well - here goes.

Enjoy!

Jean

Hello, I'm Flippin Fly and I want to tell you about my friends!

Introduction

Hello and thanks for dropping by.

My name's Flippin Fly, and I'll bet you'd love to be like me, wouldn't you? Oh, I don't mean you'd like to be a fly, but I bet you'd like to be a fly on the wall...

...at least sometimes!

You see, if you were a fly you'd be able to go all sorts of places. You'd see and hear what really goes on behind closed doors, and you could learn loads of things.

But there are certain drawbacks...

...not everyone appreciates flies!

I can understand that. After all, we do have a habit of regurgitating on the food you lot eat. That's because we don't have teeth, so we have to break it down into liquids, and then suck it up with our proboscis.

That's just a fancy name for our long mouths.

Gross, eh?

We're often blamed for spreading disease, and in some countries that's possibly true. It all depends where we've been before we land on your food...

...BUT we're not all the same.

We're just like people.

You're not all the same either, are you?

Just look at the people around you. You're all different!

You don't hang around in the same places, or eat the same food. You watch different television programmes, listen to different types of music and have special things you like doing and are good at.

It doesn't mean one person is better than the other, or if someone from a certain street does something bad, everyone else in that street will do the same.

They won't!

You can't tar everyone with the same brush as they say, but that's just another way of saying we're all different.

The thing is, often we only hear bad things, don't we? If you read the newspapers, or listen to the news, you'll hear about people who have done something wrong or behaved in a strange way.

Often, the stories will also talk about the colour of the person, where he or she is from, and what religion they are.

They're the bits we always remember, and that can be a problem. It makes some people think anyone of that colour, or from the same place, or with the same religion, could also be bad.

It's called labelling.

If you heard a story about a dog biting a postman, you wouldn't think all dogs bite postmen, would you? So, it makes no sense at all to label someone in some way and think everyone else with the same label will be the same.

Also, stories usually get changed a little bit every time someone different tells the tale. Have you ever noticed that? Just think about all the stories you've heard. I don't mean the ones in books that people read, but the ones people tell you about what they've done, or heard, or seen.

Do they perhaps change a bit every time you hear them?

Hmmm, I thought so.

Unless you were there, you can never be certain what really happened or was actually said. That's why you shouldn't gossip about people. If you start spreading stories that aren't true, it could hurt someone.

Not knowing the real truth can lead to fear, and fear makes us do strange things. Sometimes they're cruel.

People are always lashing out at me and chasing me with rolled up newspapers or brightly coloured bits of plastic, shouting, "Get that flipping fly!"

Actually, that's how I got my name - Flippin.

Do you like it?

I do, but maybe that's because I never had a name before.

My family never really called me anything. Come to think of it, no one called anyone in our family anything. My brothers and sisters didn't have names either. We just flew along together, side by side.

Well, that's not quite true. I was so small I had a job keeping up with them. I was always bringing up the rear, which means I was at the back, and often by a long way.

They say everything happens for a reason though, and one day being way behind really saved my life.

My family was quite large you see, and we used to zoom around the neighbourhood, buzzing in and out of open windows and doors. We'd check out the locations, dive bomb any food left lying around, have a quick suck, and then escape as quickly as we could.

It was great fun!

I always got there last, usually just as the others were about to leave.

That was partly because I was so slow, but also because I was a lot more cautious than the others. I'd carefully check the place out to make sure it was safe before I flew into somewhere I'd never been before.

The others were always teasing me. They thought I was a bit of a coward and checking around was just a waste of time, but one day being careful saved my life.

It was a hot and windy day I remember, and my little wings were really tired as I tried in vain to keep up with the rest of the gang. By the time I eventually caught up with my family, it was too late.

They were ALL dead!

In the distance, I'd watched them enter a big old house through the open front door. It looked really inviting, and had plenty of rooms to explore.

Several of the windows were open, including the one in the kitchen. Even though I was way behind the others, I could smell the delicious aromas wafting out. They were being carried on the breeze, and were irresistible.

I couldn't wait to get there.

Clearly my family thought the same thing. They all rushed to the source of the smells. They didn't look left or right, and gave no thought to anything other than what delicious food could possibly be in the kitchen.

They had no sense of danger.

Unlike me, who always checks carefully before entering a room, they zoomed straight into the house. They didn't seem to notice the cook who was busy preparing lunch. She wasn't expecting visitors, and seeing a load of flies buzzing around her kitchen didn't make her very happy.

The dumpy woman who didn't look anything like the glamorous cooks you see on television quickly covered her food. Then she made shooing noises as she waved her tea towel around in the air trying to swat my family.

I told you they were fast though, and she couldn't get them.

So she changed her plan, and before going to the cupboard to get the fly spray, she shut the door and kitchen window.

There was no escape!

Seeing me outside in the garden, my family tried to get through the clear glass, but of course they couldn't.

I'd warned them hundreds of times they couldn't fly through glass windows, so they must always make sure they had another escape route, but of course they never listened to me.

Now, it was too late!

Scared and desperate, my brothers and sisters kept thudding against the smooth glass as they charged towards it at full force.

It was no use, and I watched in horror as behind them a small metal can of fly spray was aimed menacingly in their direction.

In that instant my life changed forever. I no longer had a family, and I must admit I wondered if their final thoughts had been they wished they'd listened to me. I may be small, but I do have a voice, and sometimes I can be very sensible.

Everyone deserves to be heard. Even people who don't communicate in a way most people think of as language still have a voice.

Maybe, you know some people who are deaf, or have learning difficulties and special needs? Or perhaps someone you know has a speech disorder or speaks a different language?

They all have a voice, but it's just different from yours.

But now back to the kitchen. What could I do?

Well, when the coast was clear, I flew into the house and rested on the top of the kitchen door, which the cook had now opened. Sadly, I glanced down at the window sill. There was no sign of my brothers and sisters, and I guessed they'd already been scooped up and plonked in the dustbin.

The cook had also disappeared.

Upset and exhausted, I scanned the room and spotted a few tiny crumbs of food on the floor. The cook had obviously missed them when she was clearing up.

As hungry as I was, I didn't dare investigate them straight away. I was afraid she would come back, and also I wanted to make sure the chemicals from the fly spray had disappeared.

Actually, I'm really surprised the woman used that in the kitchen when food was around. I know she'd covered the food up, but even so, chemicals are nasty things and they linger.

I guess the spray was quicker and less messy than squashing my entire family against the window, though.

I'm not sure if you know this, but when you see a lot of flies together it's called a *business,* and with one press of her finger, that cook had wiped out my family business! Cruel, eh?

Not wanting to follow the same fate, I cautiously looked around and listened carefully to make sure it was safe. Then I flew down for a feast.

As sad as I was, I have to admit the food tasted delicious, but it certainly wasn't worth dying for. Why couldn't that woman just have opened the window to let my family out? They would have gladly gone, but it just goes to show not everyone is nice.

Some people never give others a chance, and life can be pretty hard sometimes.

Why didn't they listen?

Flippin Fly Poem

Do you know why
I'm called Flippin Fly?
At least I think that's my name.
'Cause whenever I'm out
It's what people shout
As they chase me as if it's a game.

They lash out at will
And it takes all my skill
To avoid being knocked on the head.
Why can't they say "Hi
How are you little fly?"
And just be friendly instead?

But sadly I find
Not everyone's kind.
Some people just aren't very nice.
If they'd get to know me
They might act differently,
And listen to Flippin's advice.

My message is clear
To all who will hear.
Treat everyone you meet as a friend.
We all share this earth
And all have our worth.
So please be nice 'till the end.

Jodi, Ben and Alex

So, that's my story. It explains how I came to this big old house, which I now call my home. I couldn't face the big world on my own after the loss of my family, so I just stayed.

Of course I kept out of the way of the cook, but she left soon after the spray incident. That's because the house is rented, and she moved on when her employer relocated.

I'm so glad she did, because the new tenants are lovely. They are three lads with learning disabilities and their names are Jodi, Ben and Alex.

I guess I should really say Ben, Jodi and Alex if I'm going by their ages, but Jodi, Ben and Alex seems to roll off the tongue better, doesn't it?

Of course the three lads don't live in the house on their own. They have support, and it's surprising what they can do. I'll tell you a bit about them and you'll see for yourself.

Now you probably know there are people with physical and mental disabilities in every country of the world, and sometimes they're pretty vulnerable. That means they're easy targets for verbal and physical abuse. Some people say nasty things about them and call them names.

Many people with disabilities and special needs get bullied too.

That's not fair is it?

Then, when they grow up, it's often really hard for disabled people to get employment or find meaningful ways to occupy their time. You see, most of us make assumptions that aren't always right.

(You don't mind me saying "us" do you? I know you're nothing like me physically, but we all have thoughts and feelings.) An assumption is a belief that may or may not be true. This is what it says about it at **www.vocabulary.com/dictionary/assumption**

An assumption is something that you assume to be the case, even without proof. For example, people might make the assumption that you're a nerd if you wear glasses, even though that's not true, or very nice.

Remember, what I told you earlier? Everyone is different!

Jodi, Ben and Alex all have learning difficulties, and I'm always amazed how well they cope. I spend hours lurking in the background watching and listening to what's going on in the house, and I've listened to loads of conversations.

That's one of the advantages of being a fly on the wall.

Sometimes, their parents and support staff have meetings here, and I've heard them say many times the three lads are very lucky. You see, until recently there was little opportunity for young adults with disabilities in UK. Most of them either went to live in residential care homes when they left full-time education, or they stayed with their aging parents.

It seems those young adults were often bored. It was hard to find suitable things for them to do, and sometimes their parents had to give up work to stay at home to look after them. That was very stressful, plus, of course, it put a strain on the family finances.

In some residential homes it was often no better. That's because everyone did the same things regardless of their age or ability, which isn't an ideal situation is it?

However, things are changing. At least they are in UK.

Many disabled people now have what is known as a personal budget. It allows them to choose how to get the best outcome from the way they spend their time, and that's exactly what Jodi, Ben and Alex have. It's a bit like when you're allowed to spend your pocket money on whatever you want instead of what someone else tells you to.

I heard one educator say the difference between the old system and the new personalised budget plan was like going to a restaurant and having to eat what you were given instead of being able to choose something you actually liked from the menu.

He said the new system was much better and helped disabled people become valuable members of the community where they live.

I thought that sounded nice as everyone has value.

Anyway, as I said, I'm going to tell you a bit about Jodi, Ben and Alex, although mostly it will be about Jodi. That's because I spend more time with him as he provides my transport.

I don't think he knows, though, so please don't tell him, will you?

School Days

I suppose the best place to start is how the boys first met, and actually, Jodi, Ben and Alex have known each other for many years. Although they're slightly different ages, they all went to the same special needs school and were taught in the same senior classes together.

In a normal secondary school everyone in the class is about the same age, and unless a student is held back for some reason, everyone moves up through the school and leaves at the same time, don't they?

However, it's not quite like that for students with disabilities at Highfield School, especially as they get older. They can stay on until they're nineteen, or leave earlier if they have somewhere else to go.

For some students, that's a good choice, but for many, staying on as long as possible is the best option. You see there's quite a lot of help you can access as a child if you have a recognised disability and have a "statement", but it gets much harder when you leave school.

As much as possible, the students in each class at Highfield School were of a similar age, but not always, and it was more difficult as they got older because the school only had one senior section when Jodi, Ben and Alex were there. Students became seniors when they were fifteen.

For those students who stayed on until they were nineteen, it meant they were in the same class for several years. Naturally, they got to know each other quite well, or at least were familiar with the names and faces of the other people in the class. Whilst not all the children found communication and social situations easy, they got used to being together.

Jodi and Ben stayed in the senior section until they were nineteen. Alex left when he was seventeen, but by then they'd all had many years at Highfield School. It was all they really knew.

Jodi and Ben had started when they were just three years old. It was only for a few hours each week at the beginning, and the school only had 38 students.

That's because the headmistress at the time was supposed to be closing it down. The authorities said there weren't enough special needs children to use it, BUT that just wasn't true.

The headmistress had more and more parents asking for a place at the school for their children. She knew the demand was there and realised if the school closed down there would be nowhere else in the area for disabled children to go.

However, the school wasn't really ideal for people with physical and learning difficulties. There wasn't much space as it was only a collection of porter cabins instead of proper classrooms, and the students had to go outside to get from one to another.

It wasn't easy, especially for people in wheelchairs, but the headmistress thought closing the only school available for them was a silly idea.

I'm sure you agree.

Most people with physical and learning difficulties find it hard to fit into mainstream schools, and for some it's harder than for others.

Often people with learning difficulties look just the same as everyone else, but because of their specific problems can sometimes seem unfriendly or do strange things. Sometimes, they're just very naughty and disrupt the class.

Maybe, you know someone like that?

Anyway, as there were more and more children with disabilities needing help, the headmistress, who was called Mrs. Ashton, worked really hard to keep the school and help it expand. Thank goodness she did!

By the time Jodi, Ben and Alex left Highfield School the students had re-located to a new school with proper classrooms, and each one was easy to access with a wheelchair.

Special rooms had been built for the children who needed quiet time, and there was a sensory room and garden for the severely handicapped.

Best of all, it was right next to the local secondary school, which meant some of the more able special needs students could join in some of the lessons there.

It was a great way for the children without disabilities to get to know students of their own age whom they wouldn't normally meet, plus it helped everyone appreciate how difficult it can sometimes be for others.

You should never take things for granted. Most people wouldn't choose to have a disability, and whilst many are born that way, in some cases their problems are caused by something which happened to them later. Usually this is through no fault of their own, but changes their lives forever.

Anyway, Highfield School had grown in size so much the new building held over 100 children by the time Jodi, Ben and Alex were about to leave, and there were enough older students in the senior section to have the school's first ever Prom.

It was a big event!

Proms are usually associated with America, so it was very exciting and unusual for everyone at Highfield School to hold one. Remember, all the students there had some form of disability, so it took a lot of organising.

The teachers and support staff helped the students decorate the school hall with an underwater theme, and the classroom looked amazing.

The teachers also prepared a buffet and arranged a disco. They were just as excited about the event as the students, and when the boys and girls arrived in the evening they all looked so grown up. Instead of school uniforms the girls wore long dresses and the boys had suits.

They arrived in various forms of transport just like their peers did who went to the normal schools. Some turned up in stretch limousines, tractors and fire engines. One even turned up in a speed boat.

Regardless of how they arrived, there was a red carpet for the students and their guests to walk on into the hall.

Everyone took photographs and cheered them on.

Many were a bit overwhelmed, but the teachers made sure everyone joined in and had a good time at the Prom. They even served food and soft drinks.

With so many students leaving, it made saying goodbye, a lovely happy and memorable occasion for everyone.

Then the students all went their own separate ways.

School was over!

APPRECIATION

College

In UK, anyone over the age of nineteen with a disability is considered an adult. Depending where you live in the country, there are various day care centres and activities you can pay to attend. However, often it means a very young person is doing the same things as someone who is much, much, older.

It's a big worry for parents.

Of course, parents worry when children without disabilities leave school, too. Parents worry about everything, but that's only because they love their children and want what's best for them. Most parents are the same. It's part of the job.

However, there's a big difference between children without disabilities and those with. Young adults without a disability usually discuss with their parents what they want to do, and where they want to do it. They make their own decisions.

There's a whole big world full of opportunities out there for them, but people with disabilities don't usually have many choices. They have to go and do whatever they can easily access, especially as most of them can't travel on their own and are unlikely ever to be able to drive.

That was the situation for Jodi, Ben and Alex, so when it was time to leave Highfield School, their parents looked at all the possibilities for their lads close to home. They couldn't find anywhere suitable, though, so for the next three years, Jodi, Ben and Alex went to colleges *out of county*, which meant they couldn't go home every night.

Alex went to a semi-residential college in Norfolk. That wasn't too far away from his home, and he used to sleep there from Monday to Friday. He went home every weekend and in-between term times.

Jodi and Ben had to go much farther. They went to a residential college in Lincolnshire. That was nearly a three hour journey for them, so they didn't get home as often as Alex. They travelled by taxi.

In Lincoln, the students all lived in different houses. There were eight in each. Some were just for boys, some were just for girls, and the others were mixed.

As they only went back to their homes at half-term, the end of term, and for some weekends, their parents used to go and visit them regularly to make sure they were alright.

Jodi and Ben stayed in different houses and weren't in the same classes. Apart from travelling together, they didn't really see much of each other, but it was nice to know there was someone they knew somewhere in the college.

It was a big thing for the three lads to be away from their families, but it's what most people do when they grow up. They leave home!

If they hadn't had disabilities, the boys would most likely have gone to college, and then on to university.

Really they were just doing the same as other people their age, but with a lot more support.

It was very hard for everyone at the beginning, and of course all the parents phoned the different colleges to check on the lads. They were naturally concerned about them, but had to rely on the feedback from the teachers and support staff to find out what was going on with their sons and whether they were alright.

All three have communication problems, you see.

They seemed happy, though, got on well, and the three years passed very quickly.

When they were nearly over, Jodi, Ben and Alex each had a review meeting. These were attended by the parents, the boys' support worker Christiana, and some of the college staff who'd been closely involved in the lads education and training.

The meetings were held to discuss what the boys would do when they left college.

Everyone agreed the boys had all coped really well living away from home and no-one wanted them to lose the skills they'd learned.

They just didn't know exactly how to make sure that didn't happen.

The college placements had only ever been for three years, so the boys had to go back *into county*. However, their parents didn't want them to go and live back home.

Well, actually that's not really true. Their parents would have loved to have their sons back with them, but it wouldn't have been a good move for Jodi, Ben and Alex.

Then, Christiana had a thought.

She knew the lads had all gone to the same school, and were of a similar age, so she suggested they could perhaps share a house.

It seemed a great idea, but could it work?

Moving On

Christiana explained a new system was just being implemented across the country to make it easier for adults with disabilities to design their own lives, and Cambridgeshire, which is where all the lads were from, was one of the first counties to give it a try.

Under the old system, disabled people had to go to places already set up, and it wasn't really working for a lot of them. The placements weren't always suitable or convenient, so the idea moving forward was to use the same funds to do things that were more meaningful and useful for each individual.

It was a personalised budget system and gave disabled people more control.

Everyone loved that idea, but knew it would take a lot of organisation. After all, Jodi, Ben and Alex would need support, not just for outside activities, but also in the home.

That was another problem. Where would they live?

Finding something suitable wasn't easy. It took a few months to find Jodi, Ben and Alex somewhere safe to live and the support staff to help them.

The place they would be living had to be close enough for all their families to be able to visit, but not in any of the same villages as their real homes. Whilst their parents loved the boys very much, they thought if they lived too close to home, Jodi, Ben and Alex would keep turning up on the doorsteps of the houses where they'd spent most of their lives.

It would be too confusing!

They had to make a clean break, and eventually the lads were lucky enough to find this house. It's in a nice village about 20 miles from all their family homes.

The house is very old, and the lady who owns it lives next door. In fact, the house has been divided into two houses. She lives in the smallest bit and rents out the large part.

That's where we all live.

The landlady has a granddaughter with special needs, so she understands the problems people with disabilities often face. She really likes the boys, and I've heard her say the lads are the best tenants she's ever had.

Of course, they have carers who live here to support them, make sure they're safe and help them look after the place, but apart from that, Jodi, Ben and Alex are really polite, friendly and tidy.

That can be a bit annoying for me sometimes. A few more crumbs or leftovers in the kitchen would be greatly appreciated now and again!

Jodi, Ben and Alex each have their own bedrooms, and share the kitchen, bathrooms and reception rooms. They keep their own rooms nice, but also have to help with the full house cleaning, shopping, cooking, gardening and doing the laundry. You'd never guess three young men live here; it's so clean and different from what you might expect.

No wonder the landlady is pleased!

The boys see their families every week and often go back to their family homes for breaks and holidays, but whilst they love the change of scenery, they're always glad to return here.

After all, there's no place like home, is there?

Different Disabilities

Their families love the three boys very much but know Jodi, Ben and Alex need their independence. They also need the opportunity to try things other people without disabilities do.

That's why their families had to let them move away.

It's incredible how well the boys get along despite all their differences. They all have varied skills and interests, and although they do lots of things as a group, they also do activities on their own.

So now you know their backgrounds; let me very briefly introduce you to all three.

Jodi

Jodi has autism and gets the most support.

He doesn't say much but understands more than he speaks. Often, he communicates by pointing and miming, and has an amazing memory.

He's got a great sense of rhythm and balance, likes cooking, art, playing the drums, trampolining, watching steam trains, painting, videos, and doing jigsaw puzzles.

Jodi's also very tidy and washes his hands...

...a lot!

Ben

Ben has Down's Syndrome. He's the eldest, and in many ways, the most able of the group. He's able to speak, can hold simple conversations, and is very friendly.

Ben loves *Doctor Who*, taking photographs, cooking, artwork and dancing. He's quite a performer and has been in many shows and had a small part in a film.

He also has a little part-time job in a cafe...

... and a girlfriend!

Alex

Alex has unspecified learning difficulties and global delay.

He's the youngest of the group, is always smiling, and speaks to everyone. However, it's often really hard to understand what he says, so Alex uses Makaton sign language and photos to help him communicate.

He loves cooking, listening to music, riding his bike, and attends a nursery every week as he's really good at gardening.

He's also surprisingly very good with...

... babies!

Living Together

So now you know a little bit about the lads, let me tell you something about their lives.

All three receive a personalised budget.

Each lad gets a different amount, and they're worked out on the basis of how much help the person needs. It's quite complicated.

Jodi receives the most because he has complex needs. Autism is very strange because people with autism are often very different from each other. Some people are slightly autistic, others have severe autism, and there's a whole range in-between.

You may hear it called the autistic spectrum, and if you imagine a rainbow, a person with autism could be sitting anywhere between each end. Depending on where they sit, they'll have different problems, and that's why you'll never find two people with autism the same.

That's also why it's so very hard to treat and diagnose.

Alex has communication problems so he has the next biggest budget, and Ben gets the least, because he's much more able than the other two in many ways.

However, in order to make their individual budgets stretch further, Jodi, Ben and Alex share the costs of the house and often do things together.

For instance, if they go to the gym, swimming, trampolining, to the cinema, bowling, to the youth club, the dance group, walking and shopping, they'll all go together. They have to pay travelling expenses so try to share as many journeys as possible.

Most weekends and evenings are spent together, but during the week they have different activities.

You remember I told you I'd mostly be talking about Jodi, and that's because whenever I go out with the lads, I usually hitch a ride on his hat. Jodi doesn't have a lot of hair and always wears a hat, you see.

In winter, it keeps his head warm, and in summer, it stops his head from getting burned. He sometimes wears a woollen hat, or a peaked one, but his absolute favourite is a special type of hat called a trilby. It has a turned up rim with a brown, blue and beige square pattern, and this makes it very easy for me to travel without being noticed.

One place I've been to on it is Jodi's woodwork class. Let me tell you about it.

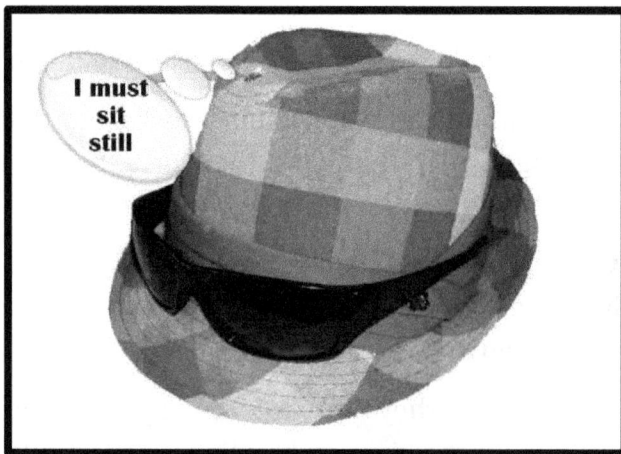

The Woodwork Class

It was a beautiful day, but as I sat on the potted plant on the window ledge looking out into the garden, I was aware I needed to keep out of sight.

The smooth white wooden sill was one of my favourite spots in the kitchen, despite the fact it was where the previous cook had wiped out my entire family with her can of fly spray. It's true that had nothing to do with Jodi, Ben and Alex, but I still feel safer hiding under the thick green leaves of the Christmas cactus plant.

A little voice inside keeps warning me to keep out of sight, and I always follow my gut instinct. It's what's kept me alive so far. Do you follow your instincts, too? Sometimes, they're very effective.

We're all living things, but I know whenever anyone sees me, they shout, "There goes that flipping fly again. Get it!"

It's such a shame most people focus on differences rather than similarities. Often it's down to fear. It happens all the time. On the bright side though, their attitude towards me produced my name...

...Flippin!

I must admit I was lonely and frightened when I first came to live here. I suppose it's like when you move, or start a new school or job, and don't know anyone. It can be scary. I'd never been without my family before, and although they never listened to my advice, they were always there.

However, the other insects in the house were really nice.

Some of them had been watching from their own secret hiding places and had seen my family being wiped out. When I turned up and they realised I was on my own, they welcomed me and invited me to stay.

It's nice to have friends.

Spinner the spider is a really good friend. Yes, I know traditionally spiders and flies are supposed to be enemies, but so what? As long as we do no harm, surely we can all live side by side, can't we?

Actually, we have lots in common. We're both on our own, and each of us hides from people to avoid getting squashed. Spinner watched his mum die, too. She met her end with a toilet plunger, and he's never been in the bathroom since.

Thankfully, Jodi, Ben, and Alex leave us alone even when they see us. In return I don't land on the boy's food (until they've finished with it), and Spinner doesn't build any cobwebs in the boy's bedrooms.

We keep away from the carers too...

...just in case!

I often chat to Spinner, and we both think even if Jodi, Ben and Alex knew we were around, they would leave us alone because they'd probably have empathy with us. That means they'd have the ability to understand what it feels like to live without their families and what it's like having to get on with different people.

Of course, their friends and families come and visit them regularly, which is nice, and I often wish I could see mine again. I never will, but I do know you never really appreciate your family until they're not around...

... even when they're really annoying!

You'll probably find that out for yourself if you haven't already.

The thing is, you always think they'll be there so you often take them for granted. When they're not and you're alone, other people can help you stop feeling lonely.

There's a big difference between being lonely and being alone, though. Some people love being alone because they can do what they want to do. It's a state of being, but no-one wants to be lonely. That's a state of mind that can be very upsetting.

If you think someone is lonely, you should reach out to them and see if there's any way you can make them feel better. Sometimes just a friendly chat can make a lot of difference.

Jodi, Ben and Alex aren't alone or lonely, and the more I get to know them, the more I like them. It never ceases to surprise me what they can do.

Every day, I follow the boys and watch what they're doing. Then at night before I go to bed, I tell Spinner all about it.

They all have different disabilities but are learning to live independently. Of course, their carers help them stay safe, understand things and do stuff they can't do on their own, but even so, they do really well.

I feel sorry for poor Spinner. He loves hearing my stories, but I know he'd rather go with me and experience the day's adventures for himself. It would be too dangerous, though. It's much harder for him to get away from people than it is for me.

I'm a fly and can move pretty fast, but Spinner can only scuttle away on his eight little legs. As disappointed as he may be, it's much safer for him to stay here in the big house with the other insects and let me venture out into the big wide world.

When Jodi, Ben and Alex go out, they either use the bus, the train or travel by car. I like it when Jodi travels by car the most.

Apart from the fact we go straight to where we need to go, it also means there's less likelihood of me being seen.

When you've got people sitting behind you it can be very tempting for them to do stuff. If you've ever used public transportation you'll know what I mean.

How many people get their hair pulled, or things thrown at them by others with no respect for personal space?

You must have seen that happen on buses and trains, especially when school children are travelling. You can just imagine what would happen if someone sat staring at me sitting on Jodi's hat for any length of time, can't you?

I don't suppose I'd last very long.

I'm sure I'd soon hear a shout of, "*Get that flippin fly!*"

I must admit bus and train trips can be pretty interesting, though, especially when we sit by the window. There's always so much to see.

None of the lads are very good with money, but they know you have to pay for tickets on buses and trains. They aren't very good at reading time schedules either. That's why they need a caregiver with them. It would be a nightmare if they accidentally got on the wrong bus or train.

Ben sometimes travels on a bus by himself, though. He works at a cafe for a few hours each week and knows which buses to catch.

He uses his bus pass to get to and from his job, and over time the bus drivers on his route have come to know him. They make sure he gets off at the right stop, and

Ben always uses his mobile phone to tell the support staff where he is.

He phones when he gets on the bus and again when he gets off. It's a safety precaution.

Luckily, Ben can talk and has been taught to use a phone. When anyone rings the house he is encouraged to answer the call, but only if he's there with a staff member. Otherwise the answering machine comes on.

It wouldn't be any good for Jodi or Alex to pick up the phone as they only speak a few words, none of which are very clear.

That's one of the reasons Jodi doesn't go anywhere alone, but it's not the only one. He wouldn't understand money, how to ask for directions or help if he got lost, and if someone spoke to him he'd just ignore them, so they might think he was really rude. That's happened a few times, so it's good he always has someone to help him.

Anyway, when Jodi goes out, I usually jump onto his hat as he goes out the door. When he travels by car he generally sits in the front seat, and I like that.

It means I get a good view out of the passenger side window as well as the front one. Of course, I don't have to wear a seat belt, which is good. I just cling on to Jodi's hat with the tiny bristles on the bottom of my six feet.

Jodi used to go to a normal college where they have a few special classes for adults with disabilities. It allows people with and without disabilities to get to know each other, and it's one way of providing more understanding of the challenges some people face.

Now, he's moved on and goes to a social enterprise scheme for people disadvantaged by learning difficulties, mental health and behavioural issues.

There are a lot of people like that around. I'm sure you've met quite a few, but maybe haven't realised. They don't go round with a sign on them saying they have a problem, and some disabilities are invisible.

Anyway, it's a lovely supportive environment where he is now, and he can gain nationally recognised qualifications. That means he could possibly get a job eventually, but of course, he'd still need support.

Jodi is gaining work skills and skills for life, but this insight is about a lesson in the woodwork class at the college where he used to go.

It was a special class with only a few students, and they had lots of help. Jodi's caregiver was allowed to stay with him back then, but now only support staff actually employed directly by the college can help the students.

It has to do with health and safety rules. You'll come across them a lot as you go through life. They'll probably annoy you sometimes, and you'll most likely say things like, "*That's ridiculous*" or, "*What's the world coming to*"? That sort of thing!

Anyway, back to the woodwork class.

As soon as he arrived, Jodi always hung his hat on the clothes peg just inside the classroom door. That was my cue to hop off and find a safer place to sit so I could watch what was going on in the rest of the lesson.

I didn't want to miss anything, especially the explanation the teacher always gave at the beginning of each class.

That's when we discovered what we'd be working on that day.

Sorry about this "we" thing. You know I didn't actually do anything, don't you? I'm only telling you what took place, but it's easier to say "we", than to keep saying "the students". It's shorter!

Mind you, I would have loved to be more hands on, or rather legs on. If only they had some mini fly tools, I'd have been really happy.

It's no good learning how to do things if you never actually do them is it?

Just think about swimming. You can read the books, listen to the instructions and watch as many other people as you like in the water, but you'll never learn until you actually try it for yourself. Remember that!

The teacher always wrote on the board at the front of the class, talked about the tools they'd need, and showed them a version of the finished product.

He always used to say, "Here's one I made earlier." (Have you noticed they say that a lot on television cookery programs? They used to say it every week on the children's *Blue Peter* program, too.)

It's best to make sure something will turn out right, though, as it would be really embarrassing if it was a disaster and everyone was watching.

In the classroom, seeing a finished product really helped the students understand what they were aiming for.

People learn more if they're given information in lots of different formats. That's why the teacher wrote on the board as well as told the students what they had to do.

There's a saying that goes something like this:

Hear = Forget

See = Remember

Do = Understand

So, the teacher told them what to do, showed them what it should look like and then got them to make it. Clever, eh?

I always listened carefully as the teacher explained about the tools and how to use them safely. Many were pretty sharp and could be dangerous if not used properly.

Of course, I knew I'd never be able to use them myself, but I love learning as much as I can. Then I can pass on the information to others. It's good to share knowledge.

You probably do it all the time, even when you don't realise.

Spinner loves to hear about the woodwork classes. Well actually, he likes listening about anything, but I made sure to explain how careful everyone has to be when working with sharp tools.

It's better to spend a few extra minutes checking things are right before you start than risk getting injured.

More haste, less speed as they say, (though who "they" are I've never quite been able to find out.) You must look, listen, and if you don't understand something you should ask questions. That's the way to learn.

"Why?" is a very powerful word, (and also it rhymes with fly so it must be important). Little things can make a huge difference, and safety is VERY important for everyone.

Each student had to wear special shoes with metal toes in the woodwork classroom at college. The students also wear them where Jodi goes now. That's incase they drop anything heavy on their feet.

I often wonder if it makes it hard for the students to walk. Their boots look so thick and heavy, and I'm sure if I wore shoes with metal toe caps, I wouldn't be able to fly.

The students wear overalls when they're working. This is to keep their clothes clean, and also to prevent buttons and loose things getting caught in the machinery. It only takes a second to have a nasty accident.

Sometimes the students put large safety goggles on to protect their eyes. They don't like them much as the rubber straps can be a bit tight and uncomfortable.

I think they look a bit like my big eyes, but I doubt they help the students see as well as I can, because I have almost 360 degree vision.

However, they do protect their eyes from dust, dirt and flying objects. The teacher said you can lose your sight if you get a foreign body in your eye. By that he meant the dust, dirt or flying objects, NOT a real body from somewhere overseas!

The students also wore ear plugs sometimes. Machines can be very noisy, and Jodi hates a lot of noise. He often puts his hands over his ears to cut it out, but if he did that in the woodwork class, he wouldn't be able to do anything.

The teacher told the students the floor always had to be kept clear so no-one tripped and the chairs had to be pushed back under the benches when work was finished.

Jodi, Ben and Alex have to do that back at the house, too.

It's good manners!

The students had to put the tools back on the shadow boards after they'd been used. The teacher said it made it easy to find them the next time someone needed something.

Shadow boards are pieces of wood which have outlines or shadows of the tools which should be hanging there on them.

Don't you think that's a good idea?

It's a really easy way to see if anything is missing.

We had to check the shadow boards at the end of every lesson, and no-one could leave until everything was put back in its proper place. Jodi liked that and was very good at spotting where tools should go. That's probably because he's good at doing jigsaws. He recognises shapes.

Also he's tall, so he could reach the shadow boards easily!

Putting things back in the woodwork class was a safety thing, but it's also good practice and a lesson to learn in life. Just think how annoyed you feel if someone borrows something of yours and doesn't put it back. I bet you hate it.

I would, too!

In the woodwork class, all the students had different disabilities, so some could do more than others. Jodi has no physical problems and good coordination, so he can do a lot. Autism is something to do with the brain. He has trouble understanding things and socialising with people. That's why he needs help.

Autism is invisible.

I've seen people approach Jodi in the street, and because they don't realise he has a disability, they'll ask him questions like, "What's the time, please?" or, "Can you tell me how to get to...?"

He never answers.

Often, he just ignores the people asking the question. He's not being ignorant, but unless people say his name when they talk, Jodi doesn't necessarily know they're speaking to him.

They must think he's very rude sometimes.

Some people have even called him nasty names. That really upsets me. Name calling is very cruel, but thankfully, he doesn't understand. He always has a carer close by now to explain he has autism.

Jodi's autism makes him very focused. He doesn't get distracted, and when he starts something, he likes to get it finished.

In the woodwork class he usually produced more than the others, and because he worked so fast, he sometimes made two of everything. He never thought that was unfair though because he likes to be busy.

The students always took photographs of their work. Jodi likes using a camera. He never seems to really focus on anything, but his photographs always turn out really good.

He copies what other people do, and when he goes out with his parents or someone else with a camera, he'll watch what they're taking photos of and will take a photo of the same thing. It doesn't matter because sometimes his photos are much better than theirs, especially his mum's!

She laughingly calls him, *"Jodi the Photographer"* after an episode of *Pingu*, which he's watched several times on DVD.

Have you seen it? It's really clever.

It's made in Switzerland and is about a little penguin and his seal friend, Robbie. None of the characters ever use proper language, but by watching their actions, and listening to the noises they make, you can understand exactly what's going on.

That's similar to watching and listening to non-verbal people with learning difficulties like Jodi and Alex. Once you get to know them well enough, you can usually guess what they want, even when they can't tell you.

Anyway, after they'd taken photographs of their work in the classroom, the students had to write about them.

Jodi is a neat writer, which is good. It means other people can understand what he's written. They can read and see what he's done, and that makes it easier for them to discuss things he's made in class and the tools he's used.

Of course, it's usually a one-way conversation because Jodi doesn't say much, but he does understand a lot.

I know that's true, and I'm always telling Spinner how smart Jodi and the other boys are. Jodi has autism and can't speak. Alex doesn't speak either. Lots of people can't speak, but that doesn't mean they can't learn.

Jodi is very good at doing practical things. He learns by watching other people, so it's very important he's shown how to do things properly right from the start. He learns by example, so good behaviour and practices are important.

Jodi was taught to use lots of tools in the woodwork class, and it helped him understand by also looking at diagrams and pictures.

He learned to use a ruler, a tape measure and a set square to measure things. Also, he used a handsaw, an electric saw, a plane, an electric drill, a hammer, screwdriver, sandpaper, nails and screws. Finally, he learned how to varnish and paint things

Jodi likes painting. He does a lot of it in the house and is always very careful not to spill any paint or go over the lines.

He particularly likes blue and would paint everything in that colour if he was allowed, but the teacher encouraged him to use other shades, too.

There are so many beautiful colours. I often think I'd like to land on the tin lids and give myself some pretty legs.

They'd be like those striped tights some girls wear in winter. It wouldn't be hard as there's always a little bit of paint left over, but I know it's a bit sticky until it dries and I'd hate to get stuck.

I'd be an easy target for a fly swatter then, wouldn't I?

Also, it would be much harder to hide on Jodi's hat if I was multi-coloured, so instead I just stick with the legs that match my body and dream about the pretty ones.

The class did make some lovely things, though. I've seen them make bird boxes, window boxes and plant holders for the garden. They've made door signs with their names on them, and because his name is so short, Jodi etched a steam train on his as well.

The class also made key holders, door stops, and mirrors. They etched their names on those, too. Jodi's was easy as his name only has four letters in it.

Back at the house there are many items Jodi made in the woodwork class, especially in the garden. Window boxes stand on every window sill, and there's a plant holder hanging from the outside wall.

It's filled with colourful plants and looks lovely framed against the brickwork.

He spent a lot of time on that.

It's made of little bits of wood all cut to the same size and screwed together very neatly in a pattern. He actually painted it brown, which was a bit of a surprise for everyone, especially me!

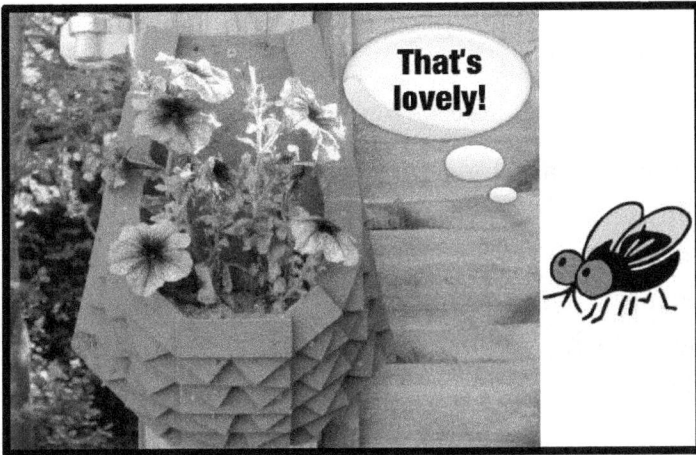

In one of the classes they made wellington boot holders. Well, actually they made them over a few weeks, but Jodi worked so fast he'd finished two holders by the time everyone else had finished one.

He painted his blue and took them home. They stand outside the door.

Each one has a flat wooden base with four large round holes drilled into it, and in each hole Jodi glued a round pole.

He'd carefully measured and sawed a wooden broom handle into four equal lengths to make the poles then had to rub the ends with sandpaper to get rid of any sharp bits. He made sure they were upright and when the glue dried, he carefully painted them...

...blue!

They look really nice.

Jodi, Ben and Alex now put their wellingtons over the poles to dry out. That keeps the mud off the floor, especially when they've been gardening.

Wellingtons are long rubber boots which people wear when it rains or when it's muddy underfoot. They're great for walking through puddles, but when you're not wearing them they often fall over and take up a lot of space, so the wellington boot holders keep them nice and tidy.

One day a lady visited our house and saw the wellington boot holders outside. The boys' boots were on them, and she asked where they'd come from.

When she was told Jodi had made them in his woodwork class at college, she was so impressed she asked if he would make two for her.

She wanted them painted purple and went on to explain why.

It seems she lived on a farm with her husband and two sons. They all had a pair of wellington boots, and as there are two in a pair, she needed two wellington boot holders.

She planned to keep them in the large utility room at the back of her house because that's where she hangs the coats and keeps the shoe rack. It's also where everyone came in from the yard and took off their wellingtons.

It was also where Shep lived. He was the old farm dog who now spent most of his time asleep, and his bed was purple. That's why she wanted Jodi to paint the wellington boot holders that colour. They would match!

When I heard where the boot holders were going, I hoped the lady wasn't afraid of spiders. That's because boot holders make marvellous hiding places for insects when the wellingtons are on them.

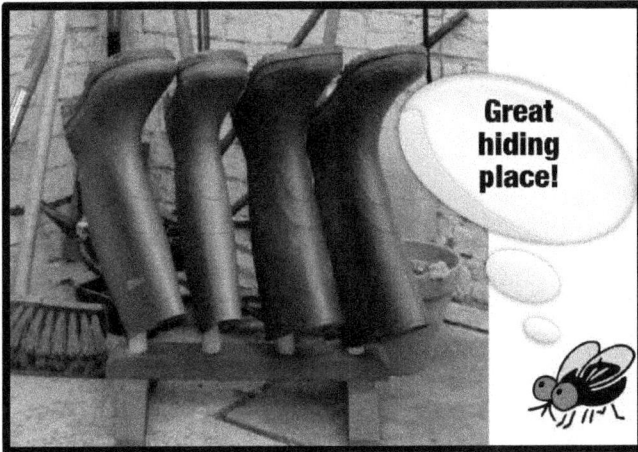

I know, because my friend Spinner couldn't wait to crawl into the bottom of the upturned boots when Jodi took his boot holders home to our house, and I guessed there would be quite a few spiders on the farm.

The lady might be in for a few surprises!

I've warned Spinner not to stay in the boots if someone wants to wear them, though. I told him if he feels the boots move or someone picks one up and shakes it, he's to scuttle out to safety as fast as his little legs can carry him.

I don't want him getting squashed. He's my best friend!

Scrambled Words

Can you find these words in the list on the next page?

woodwork class

independently

understand

friend

different

sandpaper

painting

tape measure

plant holders

screwdriver

bird boxes

visual learner

electric drill

practical

impressed

physical problems

overalls

mobility

wheel chairs

wellington boots

door stops

safety

carefully

information

classroom

special shoes

sharp tools

safety goggles

brain

questions

co-ordination

dangerous

autism

special needs

disability

machinery

focused

carefully

hammer

Can You Unscramble These Words?

1. TCILERCE IRLLD   _ _ _ _ _ _ _   _ _ _ _
2. MDPEESISR   _ _ _ _ _ _ _ _ _
3. LSVIAU RLENRAE   _ _ _ _ _ _   _ _ _ _ _ _
4. ARNPSPAED   _ _ _ _ _ _ _ _ _
5. OUADSERGN   _ _ _ _ _ _ _ _ _
6. RNBIA   _ _ _ _ _
7. RHMMEA   _ _ _ _ _ _
8. CYISPHLA RSOMPBEL   _ _ _ _ _ _ _   _ _ _ _ _ _ _ _
9. IRNINOAD-COOT   _ _ _ _ _ _ _ _ _ _ _ _
10. ACPELSI ESDNE   _ _ _ _ _ _ _   _ _ _ _ _
11. AETP MRUEASE   _ _ _ _   _ _ _ _ _ _ _
12. OALMSSOCR   _ _ _ _ _ _ _ _ _
13. BDRI BXEOS   _ _ _ _   _ _ _ _ _
14. HSARP LOTSO   _ _ _ _ _   _ _ _ _ _
15. EYSATF GGGLOES   _ _ _ _ _ _   _ _ _ _ _ _
16. ILIBDISATY   _ _ _ _ _ _ _ _ _
17. UYLCREALF   _ _ _ _ _ _ _ _ _
18. MOTLIYIB   _ _ _ _ _ _ _
19. WHLEE HSRIAC   _ _ _ _ _   _ _ _ _ _ _
20. NDDNNPELETYIE   _ _ _ _ _ _ _ _ _ _ _ _ _
21. ETDFIFERN   _ _ _ _ _ _ _ _ _
22. TPALN ERLOSHD   _ _ _ _ _   _ _ _ _ _ _ _
23. ALEICPS ESOSH   _ _ _ _ _ _ _   _ _ _ _ _
24. VREIWSERCRD   _ _ _ _ _ _ _ _ _ _ _
25. ROMANFIINOT   _ _ _ _ _ _ _ _ _ _ _
26. TANRDUDSNE   _ _ _ _ _ _ _ _ _ _
27. LAICPTCAR   _ _ _ _ _ _ _ _ _
28. WGNONLIELT OTSBO   _ _ _ _ _ _ _ _ _ _   _ _ _ _ _
29. SUDFEOC   _ _ _ _ _ _ _
30. AUSMTI   _ _ _ _ _ _
31. PINTANIG   _ _ _ _ _ _ _ _
32. EITNQSOUS   _ _ _ _ _ _ _ _ _
33. ODRWOKWO SLCSA   _ _ _ _ _ _ _ _   _ _ _ _ _
34. AIYNMHCER   _ _ _ _ _ _ _ _ _
35. IERDFN   _ _ _ _ _ _
36. TFEYSA   _ _ _ _ _ _
37. ODOR OSTPS   _ _ _ _   _ _ _ _ _
38. AELRVOLS   _ _ _ _ _ _ _ _
39. RYFCUALLE   _ _ _ _ _ _ _ _ _

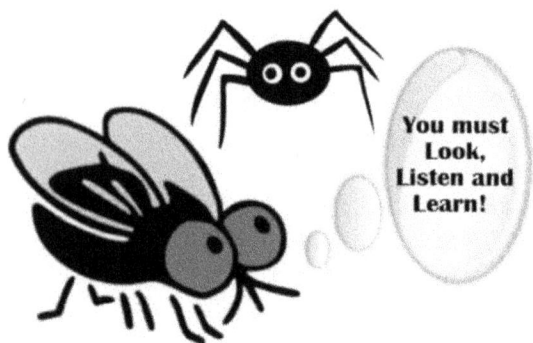

You must Look, Listen and Learn!

Cooking Class

Most evenings, Spinner and I sit on top of the kitchen door, and as I was telling him about the woodwork class I've just told you about, I suddenly heard my tummy grumble. It made me realise how hungry I was.

I hadn't eaten anything since lunchtime when I managed to grab a bit of sandwich crust a student had accidentally dropped on the floor.

His loss was my gain, but the effect was wearing off, and now the lovely smells coming from the kitchen were making me feel very hungry indeed.

They smelled wonderful.

My stomach rumbled again, and although it may have been a quiet noise to people, it seemed very loud to me and Spinner. We were worried someone would hear and look up in our direction.

We weren't too worried about Jodi, Ben and Alex, but we weren't so sure about their support staff.

Most people get upset when they see flies and spiders around.

It's strange because people are so much bigger than insects. However, fear is a powerful force. I hear it stands for *False Expectations Appearing Real*, and that means people think things will be much worse than they actually will.

I watched someone who was absolutely terrified of flying once. She was literally shaking at the thought of going on a plane but had to go because her son was getting married in another country.

For several weeks before the big day, her fear made her physically sick, and she eventually went to the doctor to get something to calm her down on the flight.

He gave her some tablets, which she put in her handbag.

However, just before the taxi arrived to take her to the airport, she took everything out of her bag, and plonked them on the kitchen table to double check she hadn't forgotten anything: money, passport, camera, phone, address book, pen, comb, tissues.

Satisfied, she scooped them all back up and put everything back in her handbag. She didn't notice the tablets had fallen silently onto the carpet under the table, and there they remained until her return.

I don't know when she discovered she didn't have the tablets she'd been relying on to get her through the flight, BUT the point is she didn't need them.

She got on the plane, flew to the wedding and back home again without anything bad happening, and now she flies all over the world.

No tablets required!

The best way to overcome any fear is to just face up to it, although it may seem really hard sometimes.

Anyway, Spinner and I sat on top of the kitchen door and watched Jodi, Ben and Alex prepare their dinner. We couldn't help notice how well they work together as a team, and that night each lad was doing something different.

Jodi had been to college, so Ben and Alex sorted out the food, and he set the table with the knives, forks and spoons.

"Don't you think they're smart boys Spinner?" I said. "They're disabled, sure, but it doesn't mean they can't do things. Wait until you see the purple wellington boot holders Jodi made for that lady who lives on a farm.

They're just like the ones we have outside the door, and I bet they'll make great hiding places for some of your little farm friends."

I saw a smile cross Spinner's face as we continued to watch the activity below

As you know, this house is very old, and Jodi, Ben and Alex are really lucky to have a very big kitchen. It gives them plenty of room to move about at the same time without knocking into each other.

Many years ago, the house used to have servants, and there are bells in the kitchen and the entrance hall.

These were used to summon the servants when the mistress or master of the house wanted something. I sit on them sometimes, and Spinner has a habit of hiding inside the metal domes.

Thankfully they're not used now because it would be quite a shock for us if the boys decided to ring them. We'd probably go deaf!

Of course, Jodi, Ben and Alex don't have servants, but they do have adults to supervise them. That's so they can live as independently as possible.

It's always good to have supervision in the kitchen, especially when there are lots of people around at the same time. It's easy to have accidents with glasses, knives and hot pans.

Whilst the three lads had their tea in the dining room, Spinner and I cautiously sneaked down. We quickly ate a few morsels of food left on the serving spoon, which was with all the other things waiting to be washed.

Then we took our places back on top of the kitchen door, just in time to watch the boys clear up. Alex did the washing up, whilst the other two dried the pots and put them neatly away in the cupboards and drawers. Each night they took it in turns to do different things.

That's only fair!

All three lads clear up after themselves as they go along. Dirty dishes are stacked on the work surface by the sink. Then, when there are enough items, one of the boys washes up, making sure not to have the water too hot.

They all know to check the water temperature before putting their hands in. They do the same when they have a bath or shower.

I know Jodi, Ben and Alex learned how to be careful in the kitchen at college. I've seen them listen to the teacher in the cooking class and watch her safety demonstrations. I did, too!

Jodi, Ben and Alex all have disabilities, but that doesn't stop them from learning. Everyone can learn if they take the time to look and listen. It just takes some people longer than others.

That's all!

I've learned a lot from going to college with Jodi. Education is so important, and I love sharing my new knowledge with my insect friends. There's no point learning things if you don't do something with it, is there?

I think I'm a good teacher, and the others appreciate our chats, but I know Spinner gets a bit jealous sometimes. I may have told you my little spider friend would love to go out into the wide world and have adventures, too, but it would be hard for him to come with me.

As you know, I always travel with Jodi rather than the other boys because I go where his hat goes. Do you remember it's called a trilby?

It has a turned up rim and a square brown, blue and beige pattern on it. That makes it very easy for me to travel without being noticed, especially as, so far, I haven't painted my legs in pretty colours!

I'm always careful to stay very still until we get to our destination, and then I sneak out and sit somewhere safe so I can see what's going on.

To be fair, Spinner could probably hide in Jodi's hat, too, but whereas I can fly away if there's any danger, Spinner would have to scuttle away on his eight legs.

As much as he'd like some adventure, it's safer for Spinner to stay in the old house and let me educate him in the evenings. Lots of people learn things at evening classes when they leave school.

You should NEVER stop learning!

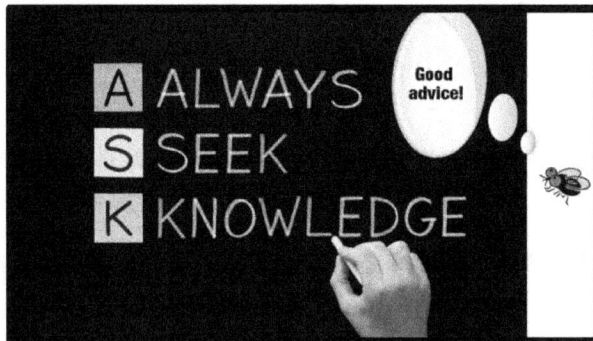

I heard one of the teachers say you should learn at least one thing new every day. She said your brain is a muscle, and if you don't use it, you lose it. I don't want to lose my brain, and I don't suppose you do either.

That's why I try to look, listen and learn as much as I can and encourage my friends to do the same.

How about you?

I love going to the woodwork class, but the cooking class is even better. Not only are there lovely smells in the room but also tiny little bits of leftovers to enjoy.

I knew the boys were going again the next day because I'd seen it written on their daily planners. Just the thought of it made my tummy rumble again. That was a surprise as we'd just eaten, and poor Spinner had a worried look on his face. We thought it would be a good time for us to leave, so quietly we slipped away unnoticed.

I wanted to get a good night's sleep so I'd be bright and alert in the morning. I didn't want to miss the cooking class!

The last session had been really good. The lads had made Toad-in-the-Hole, and I remember how surprised Spinner had been when I told him what they were making.

He thought they'd be cooking real toads and was worried I'd be eaten. Toads eat flies, you see, but I wasn't afraid. I knew I'd be okay.

You see, each week the teacher tells the students what they'll be making in the next lesson. They write all the ingredients down on a piece of paper to take home.

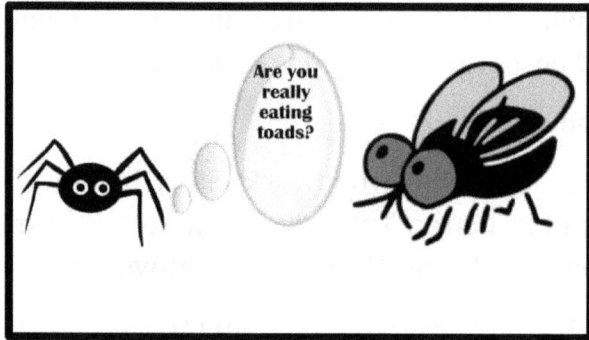

That gives them time to shop for everything and make sure they have something to carry what they make home in. No one wants to spill anything on the journey to and from college.

Anyway, last week I watched as the boys and their carer got everything ready for the cooking class, so I knew the "toads" in the recipe were actually sausages!

The cooking class is another special class for people with disabilities. As well as learning how to cook different things, the students discover how to be safe in the kitchen and prepare healthy food. I've learned a lot about safety in the kitchen from listening to the teacher and watching the boys.

Let me tell you about last week's class when Jodi made Toad-in-the-Hole. It's fresh in my mind as I've just told Spinner about it, so hopefully I won't forget anything important. Are you sitting comfortably?

Good, let's begin.

As normal, I hopped onto Jodi's hat as he walked out the door of the house. We went to college in the car, and when we got to class, I flew off and sat on the fluorescent light above the teacher's head.

It wasn't switched on, otherwise I might have chosen a different spot. However, the light gave me a good position to see and hear the teacher explain the recipe, which she'd written on the whiteboard.

This was at the front of the classroom where everyone could see it, because when you're cooking, it's important to read each step of the recipe before you start. That way you know what comes next and can make sure you have everything you need.

During her explanation, the teacher pointed out bits in the recipe where the students might need help. She always started the lesson that way. By hearing the same things over and over again, people eventually learn.

Each week, she reminds them about taking care when boiling water, using a knife and touching a hot pan or oven.

In cookery class, they had to wear aprons to help protect their clothing. They also had to tie their hair back if it was long so no hairs dropped into what they were cooking. Have you ever had a hair in your food? It's not very nice, is it?

Sometimes, they even had to wear hats. Now and again, I imagine myself wearing a hat. I think it might be difficult to keep one on my head though, as I don't have any hair or ears to hold it in place.

The students were always reminded to wash their hands before touching any food. Jodi is very good at that.

He knows you have to clean thoroughly between each finger and scrub under the nails. It takes him a long time, and I remember hearing he nearly missed a plane at the airport once because he took so long to wash his hands.

Apparently his mum had to make him run very fast so they could catch the plane. Jodi has no sense of urgency you see.

The first step in the Toad-in-the-Hole recipe was to cut up the ingredients.

The students used coloured chopping boards when preparing different types of food, and every colour was for something specific.

That's because some foods can have germs or bacteria on them, and if they aren't washed or handled properly, they can make people very sick.

Jodi's grandad had been really ill because he'd eaten at a restaurant where the same chopping board had been used for meat and salad. He got food poisoning and Jodi's grandma had to call an ambulance for him.

Anyway, the students all used different coloured boards to make sure nothing bad was transferred between the foods. They didn't want to accidentally poison anyone, especially themselves!

They put their sausages on a baking tray. Then, they added a little bit of oil.

Most of the class didn't need to chop their sausages. They just put them straight in the pan, but one student had some special sausages. They were red, round, and spicy. I thought they looked really tasty, and the teacher said they were called chorizo sausages.

She reminded the student to use the red board to cut them into smaller pieces because sausages are meat. She also explained food cooks quicker when it's cut into small pieces, and if you make them roughly the same size, they tend to cook evenly.

The boy cut up his chorizo sausages with a sharp knife. It had a black handle and I was really impressed to see how firmly he held it.

He always pointed the tip of the knife away from him and down when he carried it. That was really good. It meant no one would accidentally get cut or stabbed because you should never walk around pointing a knife at someone.

Next they chopped the onion.

Once again, the teacher reminded everyone of the importance of using different boards for each type of food. She said you can't see most germs and they get transferred from raw meat to vegetables very easily.

She went on to explain raw means uncooked, so to make meat safe to eat you must cook it.

I watched as all the students chose an orange board to cut the onion on. It's a vegetable you see. Some vegetables can be eaten raw, and many taste better that way, but it's always best to wash or peel them first.

When the students peeled the skin off most fruit and vegetables, they used proper vegetable peelers. These still have a sharp blade but aren't as dangerous as a knife.

They're no good for cutting food up though, so when Jodi and the other students use knives, they always look at what they're chopping, and concentrate hard. They don't want any cut fingers.

Jodi needed a knife to cut up his onion and as soon as he'd finished using the knife, he cleaned it and returned it carefully to the knife block straight away.

I was pleased to see he didn't need reminding. It's so much safer to have things in their right place as it helps prevent anyone accidentally cutting themselves when knives are left lying on the bench, or put in the sink.

Sometimes, if there's soapy water in the sink, or washing up bowl, it's hard to see what's in there. You have to be careful of sharp knives and also of glass things. Never put drinking glasses in water and just leave them. If they get knocked, or someone puts something heavy on them, they could break.

Broken glass is very sharp and can be very dangerous. That's why when the boys have any dirty washing up to do in their house, they put it by the side of the sink or washing up bowl and not actually in it.

Anyway, once he'd cut up his onion, Jodi added it to the sausages ready to put in the oven.

In most recipes you will see the words, "Preheat the oven". This means you have to turn it on so it reaches a certain temperature before you put the food inside.

If you don't cook at the correct temperature recipes don't always turn out right. Sometimes, ovens have lights on them to tell you when they're hot enough, but not always. Then, you just have to guess.

When they were cooking Toad-in-the-Hole, the students turned their ovens on at the start of the lesson. They were hot by the time they had their sausages, onion and oil in the baking trays, and because of this, Jodi and the other students used oven gloves to hold their trays with.

They were very careful not to touch any of the shelves inside the oven. It's easy to burn your hands and arms, and that hurts...a lot!

Oven gloves protect hands from the heat, but they need to be dry. Some people also use tea towels, but you should never use a wet cloth to pick something hot up with. The heat will go through and you could still get burned.

That's something worth remembering!

Before I came to live at the old house with Jodi, Ben and Alex, my family and I often flew into kitchens when people left their windows and doors open.

We saw many of them grab the first cloth they could find to take things out of the oven with or take the lids off boiling saucepans. Sometimes they used damp tea towels.

Often we'd hear, *"Ouch, that's hot"*, or worse, we'd see them burn their fingers and drop things. I told Spinner about that as he sometimes hides quite close to the oven, and I didn't want him getting burned or squashed.

In one of the cookery classes a girl touched a hot part of a pot and cried. I'm sure it must have hurt her fingers because I had a similar experience once when I landed on a hot frying pan. That was really painful on my feet, and they're a bit like her hands, aren't they?

In the classroom, the teacher told the girl to hold her hand under cold, running water for several minutes to cool the burn down quickly and help take the pain away.

When I hurt my feet, I tried sitting in some droplets of water left in the shower tray in the bathroom. It wasn't cold, running water though as that would have flattened me, but I did sit there cooling my burns for at least ten minutes and have to admit my feet felt much better afterwards.

Also, it stopped them from getting blisters!

Run lots of clean cold water on burns.

Back to the Toad-in-the-Hole, and when the students put their trays in the ovens, they all set their timers for 10 minutes so the sausages could cook a bit before they added the batter.

Then, whilst the sausages were sizzling away, Jodi and the other students made the Yorkshire pudding mixture. They all measured out the ingredients they needed using a set of weighing scales and put the flour into a deep plastic bowl. Then they added the eggs.

Jodi made sure he didn't get any of the shell in the mixture because it's hard to get out, and sometimes it's better to crack eggs into a jug or cup first.

He didn't have a spare one though as he wanted to use his glass Pyrex jug for the milk and water, which he gradually added to the flour and egg mixture.

Then he carefully mixed everything together using an electric hand mixer. Sometimes he mixes things by hand, but it's hard work and takes a long time to get the mixture just right.

The batter for Toad-in-the-Hole had to be nice and smooth with lots of air in it to make it rise, and Jodi didn't want any lumps.

When he uses an electric hand mixer, Jodi knows he has to use a deep bowl. He also knows to check the dial is turned to the OFF position before plugging it in.

It was really funny one week when they were baking cakes. One of the students forgot to check that, and she had the mixer turned on to top speed, so when it started suddenly, the cake mixture sploshed all over the counter and up the wall. It made a huge mess!

The poor girl was very upset, and although most of the class had a good laugh, they also learned a good lesson, (and I got a good meal).

Actually, they learned lots of good lessons that day because the teacher also told them never to reach into the mixing bowl, or put anything else in, until the mixer was turned off and the blades had stopped moving.

She also advised them never to use metal items on non-stick bake ware because it scratched the coating and made it rust. They were to use plastic spoons and spatulas instead.

Let's hope they remember.

Anyway, when the timers went off it was pretty noisy, but it was time for all the students to take their trays of sausages carefully out of the hot ovens.

They made sure to use dry oven gloves.

The sausages were sizzling nicely as they poured the batter over the top and returned them to the oven. They re-set the timers for a further 20 minutes and then began to clean up and put everything away.

The floor near their workstations had to be swept so there was nothing for anyone to trip over or slip on, and Jodi did a very good job in his area. It was very clean and tidy, and the teacher was pleased.

I wasn't. He'd cleared up so well there was nothing for me to eat!

Sometimes the students ate what they made in the lesson, but that day they were taking the Toad-in-the-Hole home to eat later.

Jodi put his in a dish and covered the top with some shiny tin foil. It made me wish I had a tiny dish for my crumbs. Not all the students are quite as tidy as Jodi, so I usually manage to spot a few.

I'd love to take them home to share with my friends.

Just like in the woodwork class, the students always took photos of what they'd made and wrote about them. They kept the recipes in their folders.

The lads have built up quite a collection, and Jodi, Ben and Alex often look at them at home. You see, on Sundays they plan what they'll eat each day the following week.

Jodi, Ben and Alex choose two of their favourite meals each. That makes six meals, but as there are seven days in each week, the meal for the seventh day is a surprise.

Sometimes they have a take-away, but for the meals they make themselves the lads write a list of all the ingredients they'll need for the week. Then when they go food shopping, their support staff make sure they buy them.

I have to say the lads cook some delicious meals. They're ALL my favourites!

Toad In The Hole Recipe

To make it you will need -

* 1 x Mixing Bowl

* 1 x Measuring Jug

* 1 x 25cm x 30 cm (10" x 12") Baking Tray

* 1 x Hand or Electric Mixer

Ingredients

* 200g (7 oz) plain flour

* 2 eggs

* 300 ml (10 fl oz) milk

* 300 ml (10 fl oz) water

* 1 onion

* 500g (1 lb) sausages

*splash of olive oil

Method

1. Put sausages in baking tray.

2. Add the oil.

3. Chop onion up and sprinkle on sausages

4. Put tray just above the centre of a hot oven (220°C /425°F or Gas No 7) for 10 minutes

Whilst the sausages are cooking you can make the batter.

5. Sift the flour and put in mixing bowl

6. Add the eggs

7. Combine the milk and water together

8. Gradually add the liquid to the flour/egg mixture

9. Beat to a smooth creamy batter

Use the whisk to slowly mix in the milk and water until all the lumps are gone.

10. After sausages have cooked for 10 minutes pour the batter over the sausages and cook for another 30 minutes.

11. Reduce the oven temperature to moderate (200°C /400°F or Gas No 6) for 15 - 20 minutes.

12. When cooked, remove the Toad In The Hole from the oven and serve with gravy and your vegetables of choice

Gardening

So now you've heard about the woodwork and cooking classes, it's time for gardening.

I told you the boys cook some delicious meals, didn't I? Well, I love eating the morsels of food they leave, or accidentally drop on the floor, especially as Jodi, Ben and Alex rarely ever buy readymade meals.

They're encouraged to eat healthily, so whenever possible all three lads cook from scratch using fresh meat and vegetables.

Sometimes, they use ingredients they grow themselves.

You see, they have a garden and also share an allotment in the village. It's great to go there and get some fresh air.

I love being in the allotment. It has all sorts of nice smells, and it's fun to meet up with the other insects living outside. I try to be friendly to everyone, and usually make new friends each time I go out.

In the house where we live, there's a large enclosed garden. Most of it is lawn where the lads play ball games, and also lots of trees and flowers grow there, which encourage the bees. There's also a little summer house.

Scattered around are some of the window boxes and flower boxes Jodi made in his woodwork class. They're filled with pretty plants and flowers.

Most of the boxes are painted brown and green because his teacher said they would blend in with the leaves and trees. They do, but I think Jodi would have preferred them to be blue. That's the colour he likes best, and they would have matched his wellington boot holders.

At one time Jodi would only wear blue clothes, but now other colours have gradually been introduced into his wardrobe, which is a good thing.

The garden here is lovely, but it's not big enough for fruit and vegetables, hence, the allotment. For your information, an allotment is a plot of land someone lets someone else grow things on, usually for a small fee, and the one Jodi, Ben and Alex use is actually rented to a lady who lives just around the corner from them.

They got it by being friendly.

One day, when they were out for a walk with their carer, they saw a lady outside her front door. She was watering some plants in a hanging basket, and they stopped to talk to her. Their carer introduced the lads and remarked how nice her plants looked. She thanked him and said the plants had come from her allotment.

Then she went on to explain she didn't have a garden at her house, but she and her husband loved growing their own flowers and vegetables. It was one way to make sure there were no chemicals on them.

She said they'd been lucky enough to get an allotment around the corner and went there most days. She was a bit worried, though, because her husband was about to start a new job and would have to work away a lot. She wondered if she'd be able to keep the allotment tidy by herself.

Most allotments are owned by the local authorities, and many people want to rent them. Not everyone has a garden you see, or if they do it's sometimes too small to grow things in. Some people even have theirs covered over so they can park their cars there instead.

Usually, you have to put your name down on a list and wait to get an allotment, which sometimes takes a very long time. If you're lucky enough to get one, you have to keep it clean and tidy, otherwise it can be taken away and given to someone else.

That's why the lady was worried.

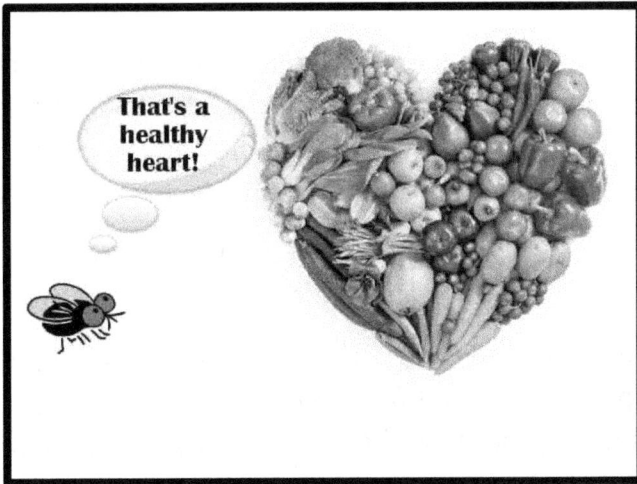

Her face looked sad as she told them how lovely it was to be able to grow her own flowers, fruit and organic vegetables, plus to be out in the healthy fresh air.

The boys are always looking for things to do, so their carer mentioned Alex loved gardening and actually works at a garden nursery one day a week.

The lady smiled and jokingly asked if they'd like to help her out. Of course, they said they would. After all, they'd each got a pair of wellington boots and a holder to put them on, hadn't they?

The lady said there were lots of allotments, so she took them to the piece of land that needed looking after. She wanted to make sure they were tending the right one.

As they walked along she explained, if the boys helped keep the allotment tidy, they could keep whatever plants, fruit and vegetables they grew. Everyone was happy.

The boys have since spent many happy hours in the allotment and are very proud of the results of their hard work. They love all the produce they grow. It's so fresh, and as they never use any chemicals, everything tastes extra delicious.

Plus, of course, it's really healthy

Alex enjoys gardening. He knows a lot about looking after plants. Jodi and Ben don't like it quite as much, but that's mainly because they don't really like getting their hands dirty.

Also, sometimes you have to wait a long time for things to grow, and there isn't always much to see. Then, suddenly, the plants burst through the ground, and it gets more interesting.

One of their carers, Jamie, went to agricultural college before he started supporting Jodi, Ben and Alex. Jamie also knows a lot about gardening and the boys love learning from him. I do, too!

Jamie has taught the boys about the different seeds and plants to put in the garden and allotment. He's also explained when you should put them in the ground as not everything can be planted at the same time.

Plants are seasonal, and it helps when the boys are shown pictures in the gardening books they have in the house. That way they know what the plants should look like and when.

Jodi, Ben and Alex all know plants need to be fed and watered. I think it's funny to feed food, but Jamie explained everything needs food of some sort to grow big and strong.

I know the boys all love watching their plants and vegetables grow. I do, too. Every time we go to the allotment, they get bigger, fatter and taller. (The plants that is, not the boys!)

Jodi, Ben and Alex take pride in their work. It helps them build on other skills, too, such as problem solving, managing projects and working together as a team.

Also, they learn about nature.

Working in the allotment is good fun, but it can also be hard work. There are lots of different activities for the boys to do.

They have to bend, lift, carry, pull, dig, plant, hoe, water and weed, and sometimes the boys get so tired at the allotment they fall asleep when they get home.

I get tired, too, and I only watch!

The allotment isn't far from the house. Of course, the boys walk there. I could fly but I like to hitch a ride on Jodi's hat because it's easier. The three lads wear their wellington boots, especially when the ground is muddy. Those long rubber boots keep the boys feet clean and dry.

Jodi, Ben and Alex wear old clothes in the allotment because they can get dusty and dirty. Sometimes, they have to kneel down to plant seedlings, or look after the plants, and the knees of their pants often get very grubby.

All the boys wear gloves. They don't like them very much, but they keep their hands clean and help protect them from accidental injuries.

Sometimes there are sharp things in the soil, like bits of broken glass, and also plants that irritate the skin if you touch them.

Stinging nettles are a real nuisance, so the boys take a bottle of vinegar with them. If you rub some on the sting, it takes the tingling away.

The boys also make sure to wear their hats when they work in the allotment and also sunscreen. They have to remember to put it on the backs of their necks and on their ears as well as their arms and face.

People often forget to cream those bits, and the sun has a nasty habit of burning them and making them sore.

The plants need the light from the sun to grow, but sometimes it can get extremely hot outside. As well as making sure they don't get sunburnt, the boys drink lots of water and sit in the shade when they can.

The allotment is quite open, and there isn't really a lot of shade, so the boys sometimes take umbrellas with them. They're useful, not just for keeping the rain off, but the sun off, too.

One of the umbrellas the boys take is a golfing umbrella. It's very big and has lots of spots on it, which always reminds me of my friend Ladybug. She has spots, too!

When we're at the allotment, I often drink from puddles and leaves, but Jodi, Ben and Alex usually take their own drinks with them in flasks because these are insulated and keep them either hot or cold.

They normally take water as it's really good for you, and you have to drink a lot each day if you want to be healthy.

If the lads ever have bottled water, they make sure to keep the plastic bottles in the shade, and never use the clear plastic water bottles more than once. Some people wash them out and use them over and over again, but not Jodi, Ben and Alex.

That's because on the bottom of most plastic water bottles there's a triangle with a number on it. If it displays the number 1, it means the bottle is only safe to use once.

However, if they do drink from plastic bottles, the boys always take the empty bottles back to the house for recycling. I expect you do too, don't you?

Jodi, Ben and Alex take special gardening tools with them when they go to the allotment. They carry them in an old rusty wheelbarrow. It has one wheel at the front, two handles and a big tray for carrying dirt, plants and other things they need to move.

It can be hard to balance sometimes, and the wheel squeaks a bit, but it's very useful.

I hope they soon realise they could put some oil on the wheel. I saw a man do that when I was flying around the allotment last week, and it stopped the noise from his squeaky wheel.

Thankfully, the boys do realise they have to be careful when they're using their wheelbarrow to carry the tools they need around, even if it does squeak. That's because they use a garden fork, a spade, a rake and a hoe to help dig and till the soil, and many of them are quite sharp.

The wheelbarrow is a great place for me to sit to see what the boys are up to. I really like to sit on the edge of the barrow but have to be careful not to get squashed when they put something in or take it out of the tray.

It's a good thing my eyes are a spherical shape and stick out from my head because it means I can see almost 360 degrees. If I see the lads heading in my direction with something, I usually move to the wheel arch or go and sit on a bush.

What surprises me the most about gardening is when the new batches of seedlings are first planted, they rarely ever look like the plants and vegetables I've seen in the gardening books. That's especially true when the boys plant packet seeds. I have no idea what they'll grow into because they all look just the same.

I know what the onions will look like, though, as the boys usually plant bulbs, and I heard Jamie tell them that the larger the bulb they planted, the smaller their mature onion would be. Don't you think that's strange? It just doesn't seem logical.

Another vegetable they plant is the potato. The boys sometimes called them spuds, which I think is quite funny.

Jodi, Ben and Alex always plant seed potatoes, which just look old and wizened. They have shoots coming from them called chits, and each one grows into a new potato.

I think it's amazing, and I love to guess how many potatoes there will be when it's time to dig them up.

The three lads always plant the spuds in straight rows. They use a dibber, which is a short fat round stick with a handle and a pointed end. It makes it easier to create the holes to put the potatoes in.

They make sure the rows are straight by tying a piece of string around two sticks which mark the ends of each row. That's because until the seeds, bulbs and plants burst through the soil, it's difficult to remember where things are.

One year, Jodi's grandad forgot to do that and couldn't remember where he'd planted his potatoes. When he went back to his allotment a few days later, he tried to plant some more in the same place. That was silly, but he is quite old and often old people forget things.

Sometimes you can plant different things in the same row, or next to each other. It's called companion planting and is a good skill to know because if you get the plants right they can help each other out by keeping pests away.

I think it's a good name for that type of planting because companion can mean friend, and friends help each other out, don't they?

An example of companion planting would be putting lettuce with other plants like carrots, onions, radishes and strawberries. That's because it only needs shallow soil to grow in and grows very fast.

Lettuce comes in all sorts of different shapes and colours It looks and tastes lovely, but unfortunately, garden pests, such as slugs and snails, like lettuce, too. These do a lot of damage in the garden, especially at night. That's when they slither over the plants and eat the leaves and fruit.

Some gardeners put crushed eggshells round their plants. That's not to feed the slugs and snails but to keep them away. Crushed eggshells are sharp, you see, and when the slugs and snails slide over them, they cut the underside of their soft bodies and it hurts.

That sounds a bit cruel to me and makes me glad I can fly.

Of course, soil has to be in tip top condition if you want plants and vegetables to grow nicely, and my earthworm friends help out there. They told me they burrow around getting air and water into the dirt, and when they break things like leaves down, it helps make food for the new plants to eat.

Worms are funny things. Have you ever seen any? They don't have eyes, ears, or bones, and are made up of segments. They can slither backwards and forwards, and another strange thing about them is if you cut a worm in half, the head end will grow again.

Weird, eh?

Anyway, worms do a lot to help the soil, but they can't do everything. That's why you have to turn the soil over when planting new plants.

Jodi, Ben and Alex use a garden fork and spade to turn the soil on the allotment Then they use a rake to make it flat and level. That breaks down the big clumps of earth, which make it hard for plants to push their way through.

The lads are always careful when they're using the tools because they all have sharp edges. Some have long handles, too.

They're also careful when they put the tools away. Jamie told them to clean them off to keep them sharp and stop them from rusting.

He also said to stand them up against the wall so no-one would accidentally trip over them.

Just like in the woodwork and cooking classes, the three boys had learned a lot about safety in the garden.

I have, too!

The lads have an old baby bath at the allotment, which they sometimes use to wash the tools in, and there's also a big plastic container to catch the rain water in.

They both come in very useful.

There isn't anywhere at the allotment for the boys to connect a watering hose, so instead they use watering cans to water the plants and flowers,.

They usually half fill these up with water at their house and then put them in the wheel barrow. Water is very heavy, and the boys can't carry it too far.

That's why they only fill the watering cans halfway. It also makes it less likely for any water to get spilled and wasted on the journey.

The lady who they share the allotment with uses a watering can, too. Jodi likes it because it's blue, which as you know, is his favourite colour.

The boys grow lots of different food. This year they're growing potatoes, carrots, onions, beetroot, lettuce, strawberries and raspberries, but Jamie told the boys they'll have to rotate the crops next year. That just means they'll need to be planted in different places.

Potatoes, carrots, onions and beetroot grow under the ground, but their green leaves show above. Jodi, Ben and Alex always enjoy digging around in the dirt to find them when they're ready to harvest. They particularly like digging for potatoes because they never know how many they'll find.

Lettuce, strawberries and raspberries grow above ground, so the boys protect them from bugs and birds. My fly friends don't bother with the plants while they're growing, but the slugs and snails are a nuisance. That's why Jamie told the boys to crush up some eggshells in a bag and sprinkle the bits around the allotment.

Birds often try to eat the fruit and plants, too, so Jodi, Ben and Alex made some scarecrows to help keep them off their allotment. They even gave the scarecrows names.

One was called Tan Man because he had a very red face, and the boys entered him into a competition at a local village show before he ended up on the allotment.

He didn't win, and although the boys were a bit disappointed, they enjoyed making their scarecrow and taking part. A huge green scarecrow called The Incredible Hulk won, and I have to admit it was pretty impressive.

Sometimes, the boys use old DVDs and CDs to scare the birds away. They hang the discs around the garden on bits of string, and as the wind blows, they turn round and reflect the light from the sun. I think they look really pretty, but birds don't like them.

That's the idea, though.

That fork looks sharp!

Jodi, Ben and Alex always work really hard in the allotment and are usually very tired when they leave. They always make sure they leave everything neat and tidy, and they have all their tools and equipment with them. They don't want to leave anything incase it gets stolen.

Not everyone is honest!

I always keep an eye on the lads when they look as if they're about to leave so I can jump on Jodi's hat for my lift home. I never fly too far away, but I love looking around the allotment. There's always so much to see and the plants and vegetables grow so quickly.

So do the weeds!

That's why the lady is pleased to have some help.

Jodi, Ben and Alex take turns to push the barrow back to the house. The wheel squeaks all the way, so I'll be really glad when they get it fixed. Everyone looks at us, and I'm sure they think the same as I do, "*Put some oil on that wheel.*"

~ 97 ~

If the boys have picked any fruit and vegetables, they take them back home and place them on the work top in the kitchen.

Then they put the tools carefully away, as they're usually clean. That's because the boys wash them off in the baby bath at the allotment before they leave, and they dry off on the way back to the house.

Clever, eh?

They wash their wellington boots off at the allotment as well. By the time they reach home, all the mud has disappeared, and they can hang them on the holders Jodi made.

Of course, the boys always wash their hands before they do anything else in the kitchen, even before they have a well-earned drink.

I love it when they take fruit and vegetables home because I can't wait to see what the lads will make. They wash them all to make sure they're clean and safe to eat, though, so sometimes I have to wait a long time before they actually start cooking.

Usually, I sit on the window sill behind the cactus plant, and as I watch them work together as a team, I always think of all the things I can tell my friend Spinner.

I also think about the delicious food I'll hopefully enjoy later.

Yes, I'm so glad Jodi, Ben and Alex help out at the allotment. It's a great way to spend a day, even if it is tiring. You get plenty of fresh air, lots of exercise, meet other people, and eventually you get some fresh, healthy vegetables to stop your tummy rumbling.

What could be better?

Gardening Word Search

```
M N R P B M I M U S D G B O U P K U Q V A G D X J B D T U G
B H N Y Y X N G Q C P I X A Y W G B J P P G O M N H N S Q H
G Z W N V Y Y C Y W U B S T T P E F P Z E E T Z D G I W T X
O C S Y T I L A E R I E U A W S N O F A A E B W F F Y E S E
T H I L E C N D J Q O L D N B E E L L L Y M P O O J N E Q B
T Y D I T F C G T S A P X J B L X W I F G O F J O E R K A Z
C G N I D N A T S R E D N U Z I E X P L H R V O I S T E P A
W G U W O S I X O N A C J D B T N D P S Z D A D J B M N F E
B U G O F W J A B Z U J W Z R M M S I T W N R I F Y N D D T
A L J P C I C A J K T I J P J P A F N N G Y S M V L G U O I
J Q F Y Z A O P B E I E R E R R J A F A K S E M Z D Y W V L
A Z Q T A P R N A N S Z I M E S D M L N Q N I N D A I F I O
M B O I A F K E C V M E M G S Y I I Y E C W T Y S I D I L P
I B Z N W U R H R M P F C K I F L L U T Y O L I E L R L L I
C L H U P N V O B S J L Y P D V K I D U T D U J I Y U S A Z
X P E T C S O L A T J F A N E A J E Z W X N C L T L B C G N
X K S R K P T I Q U L K L P N U C S V Z O B I M I I Y T E Q
E P I O U E M D W O D Q E W T I F H L E I P F Q L V H D S W
R H N P S C V A J Z A P D B I Z S O P D Z G F N I E X F U A
E O D P C I A Y N S J N L E A O J V D F J D I Y B S I J F T
H M E O B F E S O D X P A P L K A X B M T H D G A A B H F O
W E P J L I B R D F S Z B G W H D H B X U S G R S L P U P G
E S E P H E F I D E Z P O Q G W Q J E F B E N G I E F W U E
M S N A A D Q K I B O N L G Y F I C Q J R G I B D X C J T T
O L D R Y U U R R O M L G P S U P P O R T E N U P K B G D H
S O E E W W E E F E G A U G N A L N G I S L R J U U M U N E
Y O N N D S A K H Q K R Z L I Z I N R N V L A B P X E D T R
X H T T F K P N O I T A N I G A M I U F N O E V A M E M N S
X C S S S H R W M G A O B T A Z J L P Y Z C L G R O U P E Y
J S F F T H E M S E L V E S T R A V E L N O T A K A M L M L
```

Flippin fly	Jodi	autism	Ben
down syndrome	Alex	unspecified	learning difficulties
global delay	group	Makaton	sign language
residential	weekend	college	travel
parents	families	independent	themselves
somewhere	villages	understanding	tenants
polite	tidy	carers	support
homes	breaks	holidays	opportunity
disabilities	together	daily lives	imagination
reality	series	disabled	schools

Activities

I hope you're enjoying learning a bit about Jodi, Ben and Alex and I'm so grateful to have found this old house so I can share things with you.

Of course, I wish my family was still around to enjoy it with me, but I have many friends hidden away in the nooks and crannies.

We're all glad Jodi, Ben and Alex live here so we can watch them... even if it is from a distance!

This house lends itself to parties. It's big and has a lovely wide staircase with a huge mirror on the top landing. Jodi loves watching himself in it as he comes down the stairs and usually gives his reflection a quick smile as he descends the steps.

In the dining room, there's a big wooden table which is used for all sorts of games, arts and crafts and for displaying food when the lads have guests around.

Last week, the boys spread it with old newspaper and painted some garden gnomes. Alex decided to give his little figure two black eyes, which is certainly a talking point whenever anyone sees it.

They've got a running track, an exercise ball and some weights at the house, which they use to keep themselves fit. I get exhausted just watching them.

Ben wants to build some muscle to impress his girlfriend. She's got a disability, too, but is very athletic and so good at her sports they say she may be included in the next Olympics! I can't see Jodi, Ben and Alex ever being that fit, but they do go to a local gym where they use a variety of equipment. They also go trampolining once a week.

A new sports centre opened up close to this house recently and the lads go across to play pool. On Saturday mornings, they also play table cricket which is played on a table tennis table or similar sized surface. It has side panels with nine sliding fielders.

The game is played between two teams, and the table represents the "pitch". At one end, a player from one team, known as the bowler, uses a ball launcher to "bowl" a plastic ball to the batter from the opposing team, who is at the other end of the table holding a wooden bat.

The teams both start with 200 points, and if you lose a wicket or get caught out by the sliding fielders at the sides of the pitch, you lose points.

Scoring is quite strict, but it's a great way for people with physical and learning disabilities to enjoy cricket. There's even a national Table Cricket Championship, and the final is played at Lord's Cricket Ground in London. That's where proper cricket is played.

Maybe Jodi, Ben and Alex will go there one day.

What do you think?

Jodi also goes to the local golf driving range and to the swimming pool. He's quite good at swimming and has been entered into a couple of sponsored charity events.

I didn't dare go to those.

You see, I wasn't sure where Jodi would leave his hat and felt sure I'd be spotted if I just hung around the changing rooms. Instead, I stayed at home with Spinner and told him about the time I'd had to soak my feet in the shower because I'd burned them on a pan.

Spinner doesn't like water and hates showers. That's because it's where his mother met her untimely end.

It seems the drain in the shower tray was blocked, so the lady of the house decided to use the sink plunger to clear it. She stored the plunger in the cupboard under the sink and had used it many times before.

It's just basically a wooden stick with a rubber bit on the end, and to use it, you cover the drain completely with the rubber. Then you push and pull on the handle very quickly so it creates a suction and unblocks whatever is down the drain.

Unfortunately, that day Spinner's mother was hiding in the rubber bit of the plunger, and didn't have time to escape before she found herself in the shower.

She knew what was coming, so tried to get out before she got sucked up. However, the lady was frightened of spiders and was so surprised and shocked to see Spinner's mum, she dropped the plunger on top of her little body and that was that.

No more Spinner's mum!

It's so true - life can change in an instant!

All the lads have to keep the house clean and tidy and take turns using the vacuum cleaner in the main rooms, but they have to clean their own bedrooms.

They also do their own washing and ironing, under supervision of course. The support staff always keeps an eye on Jodi as he has a habit of putting the washing machine on when there's only a few things to wash.

He hates dirty clothes!

Every week the three lads go food shopping together. They tend to use the same supermarket and have a reward card so they can build up the loyalty points.

These come in really handy especially at Halloween and Christmas, which is when the lads have special parties here.

Lots of people come round and some even help to decorate the place.

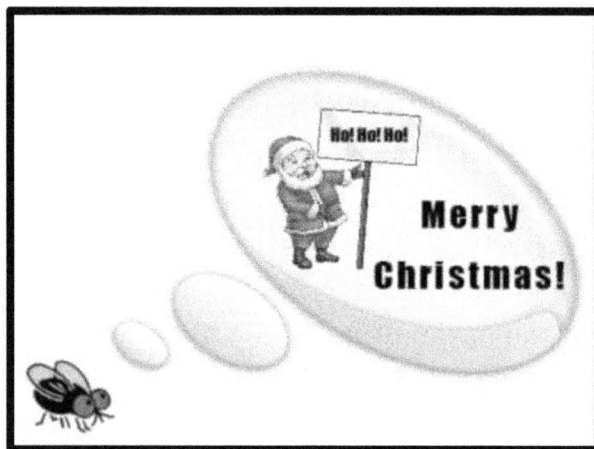

For the last few years at the beginning of December, the lads have held a party and instructed their guests to bring a Christmas decoration each time. Now, they have quite a collection of tree ornaments, baubles, lights and festive decorations, so it's quite a good idea, don't you think?

I love Christmas, but Spinner prefers Halloween. That's not really surprising; because it's the one time he feels he can stay in the open.

You see, the lads hang so many fake cobwebs and spiders around the house, no one can tell he's a real spider. Provided he doesn't move, my little friend just naturally blends in!

Halloween is celebrated every year on October 31 in UK. It's changed over the years, but it's when people used to believe the worlds of the living and dead merged together. In order to keep the ghosts away, people would dress up in costumes and put lights in their houses, which is pretty much what we do today.

Some of the costumes and masks are really creepy, and so are the faces some people carve on hollowed out pumpkins.

Jodi, Ben and Alex carve some great faces, but although they usually get their pumpkins a long time before Halloween, they've learned not to actually carve them until the day before.

That's because when the fleshy inside has been removed, they soon start to rot. Then the pumpkins start to smell and attract lots of little fruit flies.

I always try to warn the little flies to stay away, but just like my brothers and sisters, they never listen, so it's no surprise when the fly spray and swatters come out.

I always make sure to keep well away from the pumpkins, which the boys stand outside. That's not because they soon rot, but because it's a way of letting other people know they celebrate Halloween. It's a welcome sign for trick-or-treaters.

Halloween has only recently become popular in UK, and a lot of people don't like it. Many old people and those who live on their own are frightened to open their doors when it's dark, especially if someone dressed in a scary costume is waving a bucket outside.

It's become such a huge problem, there's now a common understanding that trick-or-treaters only knock on the doors of people displaying a pumpkin outside their house.

It's not an official rule, of course, but pumpkins are a sign they're welcome. Trick-or-treaters usually avoid the other houses. There's no point knocking on a door that won't get opened or where you won't get any goodies.

It's hard to know where trick-or-treating actually came from. On the television it said it's evolved over the years, and is partly based on the All Souls Day custom of souling.

That's when poor people visited the houses of wealthier families to beg for food. Apparently, the homeowners gave the poor people a type of pastry called a "soul cake" in return for promising to pray for the souls of their dead relatives. Then in later years, gifts such as food, money and ale were given to children.

In Scotland and Ireland a similar tradition was called guising and involved young people dressing up in different costumes. They would go to various houses and either sing a song, recite a poem, tell a joke or perform some sort of "trick" in exchange for a "treat". This was usually fruit, nuts or money.

Now, many youngsters go trick-or-treating on Halloween. They dress up in strange costumes and often carry a torch or a lantern. This lantern bit supposedly comes from the Irish Jack-O'Lantern tale.

It seems a lazy con man known as Stingy Jack tricked the devil when he was alive and made him promise to leave his soul alone forever.

When Jack finally died, he was refused entry into Heaven because of his dealings with the devil and how he'd lived his life, so he went down to Hell. However, Jack couldn't get in there either because of the promise the devil had made to him, so he had to roam the earth forever.

The devil gave him some burning embers from the fires of Hell to light his way and he carried them inside a carved out turnip, so that's how the tradition of pumpkin carving came about.

Trick-or-treaters these days are generally small children. They're usually accompanied by their parents and go out early in the evening just as it's getting dark.

They carry either a lantern or a torch, as well as a bucket, and when they knock on the doors dressed in their scary outfits, they say "trick or treat".

Of course they always hope for sweets or money to put in their bucket, and are seldom disappointed. I wonder what I'd get if I held out a bucket? Probably a whack on the head so I'd end up inside!

Jodi, Ben and Alex are a bit too big to go trick-or-treating, but they do dress up in scary costumes on Halloween. It's great fun at their parties as all their guests dress up, too. Sometimes it's hard to know who people are, especially if they wear wigs and face masks.

I love Halloween

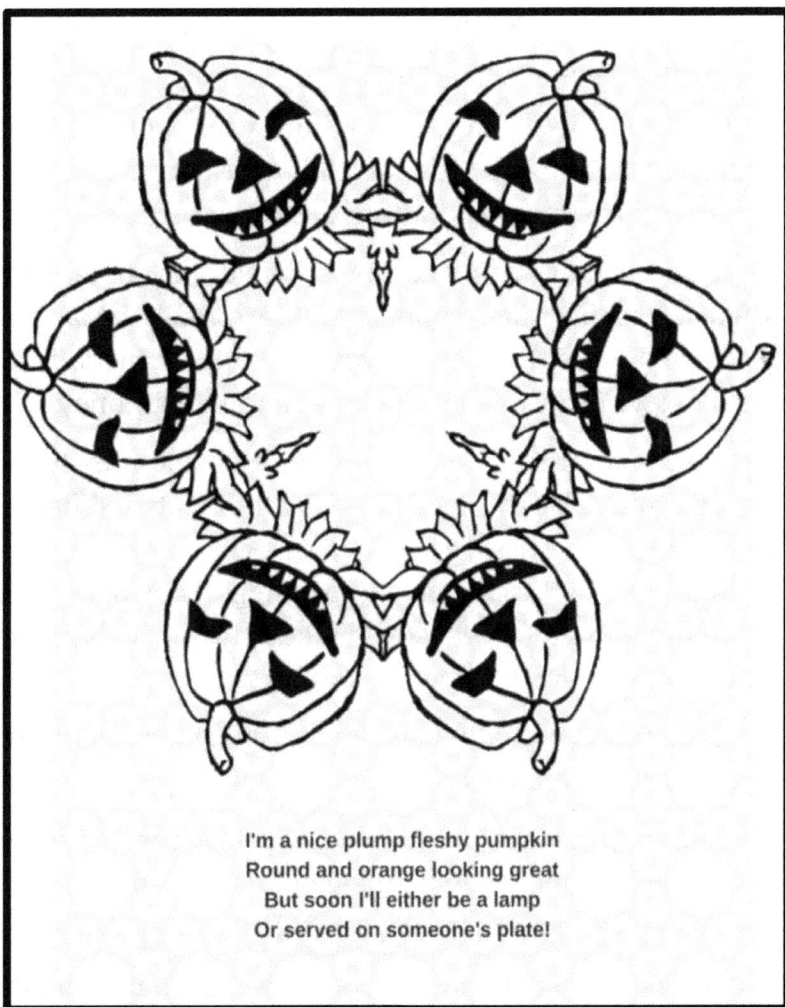

I'm a nice plump fleshy pumpkin
Round and orange looking great
But soon I'll either be a lamp
Or served on someone's plate!

Christmas is fun as well. Everyone is so happy, and the house looks beautiful with all the lights, decorations and trees!

Yes, I did say *trees,* as the boys have several. They always have a big living one in the hallway and artificial ones in the other rooms. Of course, they have plenty of decorations to make them look nice as their guests have been very generous over the years.

I guess it's true. Sometimes, if you want something all you have to do is ask. It's certainly worked for the boys as far as Christmas decorations are concerned.

Of course, Jodi, Ben and Alex would never ask for themselves, but their support staff are really proactive and are always thinking of ways to support the lads in the best way possible for the least amount of money.

They're a great team, and take Jodi, Ben and Alex to all sorts of nice places. They go to a youth club and dance and theatre class each week, go shopping, to restaurants, to the cinema and bowling. They play pool, go to the pub, go for walks and bike rides, have days out at the seaside and even go on holidays.

Yes, the boys currently have a great life, far better than their parents could ever have hoped for.

Of course, there are problems, but it just goes to show what can be done when people pool their resources and everyone works towards the same goal.

It makes me so happy to be able to share what's generally considered by those in the support system to be a success story.

As I told you at the beginning, the three lads are all very different, but despite their differences, varied skills and interests, most of the time they get along really well together.

They all have their own white boards, which are updated weekly. These act as visual reminders for what they'll each be doing every day, either individually or as a group.

It works really well, especially for Jodi and Alex, who also use picture aids as well as written words, and Makaton sign language.

In fact, the three lads are currently making a video about Makaton signs. Ben is in charge of the video camera and Jodi and Alex are the stars of the show.

For people with learning difficulties, change can be very confusing, so anything that makes life easier and more predictable is welcome.

The support staff know that and tries not to change things too often. If they do need to make changes, they apologise and explain what's happening and why to Jodi, Ben and Alex.

They know the lads haven't the language to ask for themselves, but they do understand far more than most people think.

Jodi, Ben and Alex are lucky. I know that and so do their parents. It's not always like this for people with disabilities, though, so if you can, please share my fly on the wall account with parents of other people in the boys' situation.

It might just give them hope.

Life can change in an instant, sometimes for the better and sometimes not, but one thing's certain; our reality is the result of the choices we've made ourselves, or had made for us.

Just think about me and my family. If I'd made the same choice as them I wouldn't be here to tell this tale, and you'd still be asking,

"What happened to Jodi?"

Flippin Fly Poem

Now you know why
I'm called Flippin Fly
And I hope you'll remember my name.
When you see me about
Won't now scream and shout
Or chase me as if I'm a game.

I'm just a fly on the wall
Won't harm you at all
So why should I not be alive?
Yes, of course it is true
I'm different to you
But I still have a right to survive.

All creatures on Earth
Have their own special worth
That's the reason we're all given life.
Being different's not bad,
And it makes me so sad
When it causes some people such strife.

Let's try to be friends
Before our life ends.
Being nice isn't really that tough.
Life may be unfair,
But we all need to care
About others...

...is that fair enough?

Final Word From Jean

I hope you've enjoyed this book. As I said it's certainly been the hardest one for me to write so far, simply because I've no idea how a fly actually thinks.

Still my attempt has hopefully given you a bit of an insight into how life can be for people with special needs and disabilities.

My son Jodi certainly has a far better life than I ever could have hoped for, especially when he was first diagnosed with autism. The future then looked very bleak indeed!

If you did get something from the story, and think it could help others, could I please ask you to head over to https://www.amazon.co.uk/Supported-Living-Disability-Awareness-Inclusion/dp/0955773652 and leave your personal review for me?

With so many books available, honest reviews really do help others decide which ones might suit them best.

Thank you so much!

Jean

P.S. This book is also available on Kindle and Audible.

About The Author

Jean Shaw lives in UK and started writing books because of peer pressure. She has two sons and her youngest named Jodi has autism.

For more details of Jean's other books, please visit her Author's page at

http://www.amazon.com/Jean-Shaw/e/B001K8A1A0/

Other Books By Jean Shaw

You might also enjoy reading or listening to some of my other books, and be interested to know I offer freebies with some of my publications. If you'd like to get them and to be notified when I publish any new books, please visit my site at

http://jeanshawbooks.info/extras-in-jean-shaws-books

where you'll be able to sign up.

Thank you!

I'm Not Naughty, I'm Autistic - Jodi's Journey
ASIN: B0039XRVZM
ISBN-10: 184310105X
http://www.audible.co.uk/pd/Biographies-
Memoirs/Im-Not-Naughty-Im-Autistic-
Audiobook/B00PFZRK08

Autism, Amalgam And Me - Jodi's Journey Continues
ASIN: B005GXROOQ
ISBN-10: 0955773636
http://www.audible.com/pd/Bios-Memoirs/Autism-
Amalgam-and-Me-Audiobook/B00PG3RP9K

**Mercury Poisoning It's Not In Our Heads Anymore -
Jodi's Journey Goes On**
ASIN: B005GL64BM
ISBN-10: 0955773628
http://www.audible.com/pd/Bios-Memoirs/Mercury-
Poisoning-Audiobook/B00PG3PP6A

Supported Living - Jodi's Journey Moves On
ASIN:- B0179X5KF0
ISBN:--10: 0955773636
http://www.audible.com/pd/A3CKJXX099NXKN

The GVO Story
ASIN: B005LV8M7Q
ISBN-10: 1466363983
http://www.audible.com/pd/Bios-Memoirs/The-GVO-
Story-Audiobook/B00MNJ8CUG

The 7MinuteWorkout Story
ASIN: B007IVVJC2
ISBN-10: 1470180464
http://www.audible.com/pd/Health-Fitness/The-7-
Minute-Workout-Story-Audiobook/B00OC28O1E

Concerns Of Women Over 50
ASIN: B00ID4YPR4
ISBN-10: 1477569847
http://www.audible.com/pd/Health-Fitness/Concerns-of-Women-Over-50-Audiobook/B00MHXJTS2

Jodi Goes To The Farm (illustrated)
ASIN: B00B9VVJ4U
ISBN-10: 1482316315
http://www.audible.com/pd/Kids/Jodi-Goes-to-the-Farm-Educational-Illustrated-Childrens-Rhyming-Book-Audiobook/B00JW0CB6A

Jodi Goes To The Farm (photo)
ASIN: B00GL2UNXU
ISBN-10: 1493741985
http://www.audible.com/pd/Kids/Jodi-Goes-to-the-Farm-Educational-Illustrated-Childrens-Rhyming-Book-Audiobook/B00JW0CB6A

Jodi Goes To The Zoo (illustrated)
ASIN: B00B8XE4Q4
ISBN-10: 1482316250
http://www.audible.com/pd/Kids/Jodi-Goes-to-the-Zoo-Educational-Illustrated-Childrens-Rhyming-Book-Audiobook/B00JW0DFPG

Jodi Goes To The Zoo (photo)
ASIN: B00GL2YTO4
ISBN-10: 1493741829
http://www.audible.com/pd/Kids/Jodi-Goes-to-the-Zoo-Educational-Illustrated-Childrens-Rhyming-Book-Audiobook/B00JW0DFPG

Jodi Visits The Farm (illustrated)
ASIN: B00GKKOKIM
ISBN-10: 1493721720
http://www.audible.com/pd/Kids/Jodi-Visits-the-Farm-Audiobook/B00KSKT6M0

Jodi Visits The Farm (photo)
ASIN: B00GKKOLVS
ISBN-10: 1493741527
http://www.audible.com/pd/Kids/Jodi-Visits-the-Farm-Audiobook/B00KSKT6M0

Jodi Visits The Zoo (illustrated)
ASIN: B00GKKSEAM
ISBN-10: 1493741268
http://www.audible.com/pd/Kids/Jodi-Visits-the-Zoo-Audiobook/B00KSKSUT0

Jodi Visits The Zoo (photo)
ASIN: B00GKKOJ2Y
ISBN-10: 1493741764
http://www.audible.com/pd/Kids/Jodi-Visits-the-Zoo-Audiobook/B00KSKSUT0

Ida Godbold - 100 Years and Counting!
ASIN: B00KNW36TM
ISBN-10: 1499558783

A Life In Rhyme - My Story
ASIN: B00IC4V5T6
ISBN-10: 1495465519
http://www.audible.com/pd/Drama-Poetry/A-Life-in-Rhyme-Audiobook/B00KCRHY96

A Life In Rhyme - My Family
ASIN: B00IC5NX2W
ISBN-10: 1495492737
http://www.audible.com/pd/Drama-Poetry/A-Life-in-Rhyme-My-Family-Audiobook/B00N9CEV3S

A Life In Rhyme - People Poems
ASIN: B00IC5HWQK
ISBN-10: 1495492915
http://www.audible.com/pd/Drama-Poetry/A-Life-In-Rhyme-People-Poems-Audiobook/B00KIULCIQ

A Life In Rhyme - Life's Observations
ASIN: B00IC64EMY
ISBN-10: 1495493121
http://www.audible.com/pd/Drama-Poetry/A-Life-In-Rhyme-Audiobook/B00JMO3WBY

Halloween Fun Activity and Colouring Book
ISBN-10: 0955773644

Life and Death Matters - A Simple Journal To Tie-Up Loose Ends
ISBN-10: 0955773660

Flippin Fly and the Zoo Animal Alphabet
ASIN: B01M11O5AC
ISBN-10: 0955773679
Audio - https://www.amazon.co.uk/dp/B01N7FOV7K

Eeey Beey the Easter Bunny - A Fun Story, Activity and Colouring Book for Boys and Girls
ISBN-10: 154481254X

www.ingramcontent.com/pod-product-compliance
Lightning Source LLC
Chambersburg PA
CBHW061741020426
42331CB00006B/1319